J.R. H

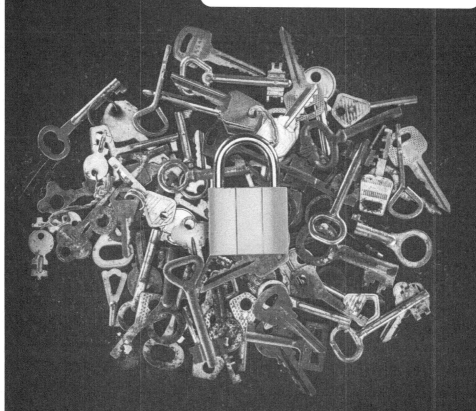

THE ULTIMATE

PHYSICAL

SECURITY CERTIFICATION STUDY GUIDE

PASS ON YOUR FIRST TRY!

The Ultimate Physical Security Certification (PSC) Study Guide

Table of Contents

As a Security Professional in the Defense industry, the Physical Security Certification (PSC) represents a follow-on certification after the Security Fundamentals Professional Certification (SFPC). Haven't taken the SFPC yet? Get our guide here: https://spedcertification.weebly.com/

Both the PSC and the SFPC are required before attaining more advanced SPeD certifications.

When I started to attain my PSC, I was a bit disheartened when I learned that there was no roadmap clearly delineating which courses to take, what order to achieve them, and what questions to study.

One would think that a professional organization like Defense Security Service (DSS) would have a Learning Plan for all of their certifications. 'Enroll in this Learning Plan and it registers you for the 13 applicable courses that will prep you for that test'. Nope!

Instead, when creating the Security Training, Education and Professionalization Portal (STEPP), they created just another database of courses where you are left to choose your own adventure.

I originally created this book as a standard operating procedure to pass down to those in my office in hopes to save some valuable time.

Since that time, it's grown to include Student Guides to all of the Physical Security Computer-Based Trainings (CBTs). If you don't feel like taking the CBT, quickly scan the Student Guide. Many times, these Student Guides are verbatim the narration throughout the CBTs. Many times, you can skim them faster than they're spoken and they are also searchable if you're looking for something more specific!

This book has also grown to include every PSC-related question that our security team could harvest. We've scoured all available resources and gone to every corner of the interwebs in order to compile the largest testbank available anywhere (we know, we've looked)!

What follows are all of the applicable PSC Courses, their associated Student Guides, and the resources and references you'll need to prepare for the PSC. They will give you a general overview of the concepts when preparing to challenge the test. When navigating to each of the embedded hyperlinks, ensure you are logged into STEPP first. If not, many of the course-specific links will not work.

Principles

These are the Security Principles tested on the PSC. You'll need to familiarize yourself with courses and directives that address these topics:

- Facility access control
- Key, Combo and Lock control
- Emergency Management and response
- Phys Sec standards for special assets and resources
- PHYSEC for classified material
- Physical Security Standards for Sensitive Conventional Arms, Ammunition, and Explosives
- Security Systems Devices (CCTV)
- Site Design Strategy
- Protective barriers
- Site lighting

Weighted Test Breakdown

Area of Expertise	
Physical Security Concepts Exam	**Weight 22%**
Physical Security Concepts	Facility Access Control

Area of Expertise	
Physical Security Standards Exam	**Weight 24%**
Physical Security Standards for Storage of Classified Information	
Physical Security Standards for Sensitive Conventional Arms, Ammunitions, and Explosives	
Physical Security Standards for Special Assets/Resources	

Area of Expertise	
Standards, Countermeasures, and Planning Exam	**Weight 41%**
Protective Barriers	
Site Lighting	
Key, Combination, and Lock Control	
Site Design Strategies	
Security Systems Devices	

Area of Expertise	
Physical Security Planning and Implementation Exam	**Weight 13%**
Physical Security Planning and Plan Implementation	
Emergency Management/Emergency Response	

Applicable E-Learning Courses and Resources

These courses are a good start for preparing for the PSC. Just going through the CBTs, taking a few notes and reviewing them before the test was enough to pass for me.

When preparing for the exam, skimming the instructions/directives/resources (even if it's just the table of contents to know what *type of material* is covered in each publication) proved to be very valuable. It helped me make better educated guesses once I whittled answers down to just a few viable options.

At a minimum, you should plan on either taking the CBT or reading through the Student Guide which is typically an exact transcript of what is delivered. Courses can be accessed through your STEPP account (https://stepp.dss.mil/SelfRegistration/Login.aspx). Once you're logged into STEPP, THEN CLICK the REGISTER links below.

Introduction to Physical Security Course, PY011.16
REGISTER:

https://stepp.dss.mil/Sumtotal82/app/management/LMS_ActDetails.aspx?ActivityId=258113

Intro to Physical Security Student Guide

- DoD 5200.08-R - Physical Security Program
- ICD 705 - Sensitive Compartmented Information Facilities
- DoDD 3020.40 - Mission Assurance (MA)
- DoDD 5205.07 - Special Access Program (SAP) Policy
- DoDI 2000.12 - DoD Antiterrorism (AT) Program
- **DoDI O-2000.16 - DoD Antiterrorism (AT) Standards**
  - Volume 1 Requires CAC
  - Volume 2 Requires CAC
- DoDI 5200.08 - Security of DoD Installations and Resources and the DoD Physical Security Review Board (PSRB)
- DoDI O-5210.63 - DoD Procedures for Security of Nuclear Reactors and Special Nuclear Materials (SNM)Requires CAC
- DoDI 5210.65 - Security Standards for Safeguarding Chemical Agents
- DoDI 5210.84 - Security of DoD Personnel at U.S. Missions Abroad
- DoDM 5200.01 Vol. 1-4 - DoD Information Security Program
  - Volume 1, Volume 2, Volume 3 , Volume 4
- DoD S-5210.41M - Nuclear Weapon Security Manual: DoD Nuclear Weapon Environment-Specific Requirements (U) content available on SIPRnet
- DoD 5220.22M - National Industrial Security Program Operating Manual (NISPOM)

Physical Security Measures, PY103.16
REGISTER:
https://stepp.dss.mil/Sumtotal82/app/management/LMS ActDetails.aspx?ActivityId=44192

Physical Security Measures Student Guide

- DoD 5200.08-R - Physical Security Program
- DoD 5220.22M - National Industrial Security Program Operating Manual (NISPOM)
- DoDI 8520.02 - Public Key Infrastructure (PKI) and Public Key (PK) Enabling
- DoDM 5100.76 - Physical Security of Sensitive Conventional Arms, Ammunition, and Explosives (AA&E)
- DoDM 5200.01 Vol. 1-4 - DoD Information Security Program
  - Volume 1, Volume 2, Volume 3 , Volume 4
- Homeland Security Presidential Directive 12 (HSPD-12)

Physical Security Planning and Implementation PY106.16
REGISTER:
https://stepp.dss.mil/Sumtotal82/app/management/LMS ActDetails.aspx?ActivityId=264725

Physical Security Planning and Implementation Student Guide

- ATTP 3-39.32 - Physical Security
- DoD 5200.08-R - Physical Security Program
- DoDD 3020.26 - Defense Continuity Program
- DoDD 3020.40 - DoD Policy and Responsibilities for Critical Infrastructure

- DoDI 2000.12 - DoD Antiterrorism (AT) Program
- DoDI 2000.16 - DoD Antiterrorism (AT) Standards
- DoDI 5200.08 - Security of DoD Installations and Resources and the DoD Physical Security Review Board (PSRB)
- DoDM 5200.01 Vol. 1-4 - DoD Information Security Program
  - Volume 1, Volume 2, Volume 3 , Volume 4
- Executive Order 12656
- Joint Knowledge Online
- Military Handbook 1013/10
- Military Handbook 1013/1A

Electronic Security Systems PY250.16

REGISTER:

https://stepp.dss.mil/Sumtotal82/app/management/LMS_ActDetails.aspx?ActivityId=262859

Electronic Security Systems Student Guide

- Homeland Security Presidential Directive (HSPD) 12: Policy for a Common Identification Standard for Federal Employees and Contractors, 27 August 2004
- Unified Facilities Criteria (UFC) 4-021-02, Electronic Security Systems, 1 October 2013
- Unified Facilities Criteria (UFC) 4-010-05, Sensitive Compartmented Information Facilities Planning, Design, and Construction, 1 October 2013
- DoD 5200.08-R, DoD Physical Security Program, 9 April 2007
- DoDM 5105.21, Vol. 1-3, Sensitive Compartmented Information Administrative Security Manual
  - Volume 1
  - Volume 2
  - Volume 3
- DoDM 5200.01, Vol. 3, DoD Information Security Program
- DoDM 5100.76, Physical Security of Sensitive Conventional Arms, Ammunition, and Explosives
- ICD 705, Sensitive Compartmented Information Facilities, 26 May 2010
- IC Tech Spec for ICD/ICS 705, Technical Specifications for Construction and Management of Sensitive Compartmented Information Facilities, 23 April 2012
- ICS 705-1, Physical and Technical Security Standards for Sensitive Compartmented Information Facilities, 17 September 2010
- ICS 705-2, Standards for the Accreditation and Reciprocal Use of Sensitive Compartmented Information, 17 September 2010
- Identity, Credential & Access management

Exterior Security Lighting PY109.16

REGISTER:

https://stepp.dss.mil/SumTotal82/lang-en/management/LMS_ActDetails.asp?ActivityId=265441

Exterior Security Lighting Student Guide

- ATTP 3-39-32 Army Tactics, Techniques, and Procedures, "Physical Security"
- UFC 3-530 01 Design: Interior, Exterior Lighting and Controls
- UFC 4 022 01 Security Engineering Entry Control Facilities / Access Control Points
- DoDM 5100.76 Physical Security of Sensitive Conventional Arms, Ammunition, and Explosives (AA&E)

Lock and Key Systems PY104.16
REGISTER:

https://stepp.dss.mil/Sumtotal82/app/management/LMS_ActDetails.aspx?ActivityId=264724

Lock and Key Systems Student Guide

- Lock Videos/Job Aids
  - Operating and Closing X-10 Electromechanical Combination Lock
  - Changing Combination of X-10 Electromechanical Combination Lock
  - Operating the S&G 2740B Electromechanical Safe Lock
  - Changing Combination of S&G 2740B Electromechanical Safe Lock
  - Operating X-07 and X-09 Locks
  - Changing Combination of X-07 and X-09 Locks
  - Operating S&G 2740 Locks
  - Changing Combination of S&G 2740 Locks
- DoD 5200.08-R - Physical Security Program
- DoD 5220.22M - National Industrial Security Program Operating Manual (NISPOM)
- DoD Lock Program
- DoDI 5200.08 - Security of DoD Installations and Resources and the DoD Physical Security Review Board (PSRB)
- DoDM 5100.76 - Physical Security of Sensitive Conventional Arms, Ammunition, and Explosives (AA&E)
- DoDM 5200.01 Vol. 1-4 - DoD Information Security Program
  - Volume 1, Volume 2, Volume 3 , Volume 4
- FF-L-2740B June 15, 2011 Superseding FF-L-2740A January 12, 1997
- FF-L-2740B Amendment 1 May 2, 2012
- FF-L-2937 January 31, 2005
- FF-P-110J February 11, 1997 Superseding FF-P-110H March 11, 1994
- FF-P-110J Amendment 120 January 2004
- FF-P-2827A March 30 1999
- FF-P-2827A Amendment 1 August 2, 2004
- MIL-DTL-29181C March 10, 1998
- MIL-DTL-43607J July 29, 2010

Storage Containers and Facilities PY105.16
REGISTER:

https://stepp.dss.mil/Sumtotal82/app/management/LMS_ActDetails.aspx?ActivityId=264941

Storage Containers and Facilities Student Guide

- AA-C-2859A - Cabinet, Security, Weapons Storage
- AA-D-600D - Door, Vault, Security
- AA-D-600D Amendment 4 - Door, Vault, Security - January 5, 2010
- AA-V-2737 Modular Vault Systems
- AA-V-2737 Amendment 3 Modular Vault Systems - February 25, 2013
- DoD 5220.22M - National Industrial Security Program Operating Manual (NISPOM)
- DoDM 5100.76 - Physical Security of Sensitive Conventional Arms, Ammunition, and Explosives (AA&E)
- DoDM 5200.01 Vol. 1-4 - DoD Information Security Program
  - Volume 1, Volume 2, Volume 3 , Volume 4
- DoD S-5210.41M - Nuclear Weapon Security Manual: DoD Nuclear Weapon Environment-Specific Requirements (U)
- FF-L-2740B June 15, 2011 Superseding FF-L-2740A January 12, 1997
- FF-L-2740B Amendment 1 May 2, 2012
- FF-P-110J February 11, 1997 Superseding FF-P-110H March 11, 1994
- FF-P-110J Amendment 120 January 2004
- MIL-DTL-43607J July 29, 2010
- SF700 - Security Container Information
- SF701 - Activity Security Checklist
- SF702 - Security Container Check Sheet

Physical Security Virtual Environment Assessment PY108.06
REGISTER: https://stepp.dss.mil/Sumtotal82/app/management/LMS_ActDetails.aspx?ActivityId=258114

This training serves as a capstone assessment for the Physical Security courses offered by the CDSE. The previous seven courses are required as prerequisites.

- DoD 5200.08R Physical Security Number Program April 9, 2007 Incorporating Change 1, May 27, 2009
- DoDI 5200.08 Security of DoD Installations and Resources
- ATTP 3-39.32 Physical Security Army Tactics techniques and Procedures
- MIL-HDBK-1013-10 Design Guidelines for Security Fencing, Gates, Barriers, and Guard Facilities, 14 May 1993
- Department of Defense Manual Number 5100.76 April 17, 2012
- DoD Lock Program
- DoDM 5200.01, Volumes 1-4 (DoD Information Security Program)
  - Volume 1, Volume 2, Volume 3 , Volume 4

Antiterrorism Officer (ATO) Level II GS109.16
REGISTER:
https://stepp.dss.mil/Sumtotal82/app/management/LMS_ActDetails.aspx?ActivityId=277429

I'm not sure how valuable this training is with regards to PSC. I took the ATO Level II course in person a couple years back and did not complete this CBT.

- Acquisition Community Connection
- Air Force Instruction 10-245 - Air Force AT Standards
- Antiterrorism Enterprise Portal (ATEP)
- DoDI 2000.12 - DoD Antiterrorism Program
- DoDI 2000.16 - DoD Antiterrorism Standards
- DoDI 2000.26 - Suspicious Activity Reporting
- DoDI 3020.52 - DoD Installation CBRNE Preparedness Standards
- DoD Regulation 5200.8-R - Physical Security Program
- DoD Support to International Chemical, Biological, Radiological, and Nuclear (CBRN) Incidents
- guardian System
- LEEP - Law Enforcement Enterprise Portal
- NCTC - National Counterterrorism Center
- NJTTF - National Joint Terrorism Task Force
- POM - Program Objective Memorandum
- SAR Line Officer Training Video
- State Department website

Risk Management for DoD Security Programs GS102
REGISTER: https://stepp.dss.mil/SumTotal82/lang-en/management/LMS_ActDetails.asp?ActivityId=208

Risk Management for DoD Security Programs Student Guide

- Job Aid - Risk Management Tables/Charts/Worksheets

Question Answering Strategy
The PSC assessment used three basic types of questions: (1) multiple-choice with one correct answer, (2) convergent true-or-false and (3) Multiple Response.

1. Multiple-Choice. A multiple-choice item includes a question and a number of options listed as potential answers. In this type of question, your task is to choose the option that correctly answers the presented question.

Which of the following is NOT a physical security measure?

A. Perimeter fences
B. Security guards
C. Marking classified documents
D. Alarm systems

2. Convergent True-or-False. A convergent true-or-false question consists of an item stem that: (1) identifies the general topic area being addressed by the item, and (2) presents two statements regarding that topic area. It then asks the respondent to determine if one or both of the statements are correct or incorrect with respect to the topic area.

> Two security professionals, **Brian and Melissa**, are discussing certification and accreditation (C&A) for Storage of Classified DoD Information Systems. **Brian says** that the DoD Manual 5100.76M governs the C&A for Storage of Classified DoD Information Systems. **Melissa says** that Designated Accrediting Authority (DAAs) have the authority and responsibility for accreditation decisions.
>
> Who is correct?
>
> A. Brian is correct
> B. Melissa is correct
> C. Brian and Melissa are both correct
> D. Brian and Melissa are both incorrect

3. Multiple Response. A Multiple Response question is identical to a Multiple-Choice question, except there could be more than one correct answer. How do you tell the difference? Multiple Response questions will have "Choose all that apply" in the instructions. Many questions on the test will challenge a deeper breadth of material than what is presented in the CBTs.

> Which of the following does a physical security program aim to prevent unauthorized access to (Choose all that apply)?
>
> ☐ Personnel
> ☐ Equipment
> ☐ Installations
> ☐ Information

These different types of questions will require different answering strategies. The Student Integrity Pledge won't allow me to tell you the specific questions that were on my test, but the test bank below and the CBT courses above just about cover it all.

You'll need to know a lot of 'lists. As you take the CBT courses or skim the Student Guides, write down any 'lists. For example, in the *Introduction to Risk Management Course* you should note:

- The 5 Steps of Risk Management Model
- The 4 Identification levels of Assets and Threats (Crit/High/Med/Low)

- The 5 General Types of Vulnerabilities (Human, Operational, Information, Facility, Equipment)
- The 3 Types of Countermeasures (Manpower, Equipment, Procedural)

Then review **those** before you walk into your test. It will help frame the topics in your mind so you know what 'sounds right' and what doesn't. You'll be glad you did when you're on your 20th "Convergent True-or-False" and you're thinking to yourself that Brian and Melissa are both idiots. More Course-Specific Lists at the end of this section.

As you go through the test, completely read the test question. Then as you go through each answer, quickly determine if it 'sounds right' or 'sounds bogus'. Doing this allowed me to whittle down many questions to just two answers. Even questions that asked about parts of security I've never been involved in (there's a LOT of AA&E), I was able to make an educated guess.

When you get down to just two answers, pick the answer that is MOST right. There were a couple questions that I swore I knew the answer to, but felt I was presented with two correct answers. Select the MOST correct answer. Look for absolute words like 'always', 'never' and 'required'. Those are the easiest to dismiss.

Specifically, you'll need to know response times for security personnel responding to SCIF alarms (both SCIFs that have 'security in depth' and SCIFs that do not). There were a lot of AA&E questions, I should have at least skimmed those resources more (or not been so dismissive of those types of question/answers in the test bank). You'll need to know the random requirements to inspect crates that are delivered to a squadron when banded and when unbanded (What % do you have to check? What % of inventory should you check in the crate? How long should you keep the inspection records?), that kind of stuff.

As you go through the Test Bank below, if there's a question that you're absolutely clueless about, skim the resource or directive. Spend about 5 minutes reading just the pages or sections concerned with that topic.

More Lists

Introduction to Physical Security Course, PY011.16

- 6 Types of DoD Assets (Personnel, Information, Equipment, Facilities, Activities, Operations) (PIEFAO)
- The duties and responsibilities of the Physical Security Coordinating Activities (ATEC, ATWG, ISO, SJA, TWG)
- Duties and Responsibilities of the Individuals (Installation CDR, ATO, CI Support, local/state/fed LEO, OPSEC-O, PHYSEC-O)
- Threats vs Vulnerabilities vs Criticality

Physical Security Measures, PY103.16

- 3 Barrier Systems (Active, Passive/Fixed, Natural)
- Types of lighting (again)
- IDS Operational Phases (Detection, Reporting, Dispatch, Response/assessment)
- Types of Monitoring (Local, Proprietary, Central Station)

Physical Security Planning and Implementation PY106.16

- 5 Threats to DoD Assets and Operations (Criminal, Foreign Intel Activities, Natural Disasters, Insider Threat, Terrorists)
- 2 Types of Inspections
- 5 Types of Plans (Physical Security Plan, Standard Operating Procedure, Post Orders, COOP, MOA/MOU)
- A man-passable opening is anything greater than 96square"
- Point Security vs Area Security

Electronic Security Systems PY250.16

- 5 Functions of IDS (Deter, Detect, Document, Deny, Delay)
- Type of Interior IDS and Types of Exterior IDS
- Differentiate the Types of Access Control Systems (Manual, Manual w/ Automated Electronics, Automated)
- Examples of Screening Equipment

Lock and Key Systems PY104.16

- 3 types (Combo, Mechanical, Combo Padlock) and classification level
- Differentiate Methods of Storage (Secure Room, Vaults, SCIF, Security Container)
- Types of Lock actual locks that in compliance (FF-L-2740 series, X-10, CDX-10, S&G2740B, S&G2890PDL, S&G2937/FF-L-2937)

Risk Management for DoD Security Programs GS102

- The 5 Steps of Risk Management Model
- The 4 Identification levels of Assets and Threats (Crit/High/Med/Low)
- The 5 General Types of Vulnerabilities (Human, Operational, Information, Facility, Equipment)
- The 3 Types of Countermeasures (Manpower, Equipment, Procedural)

Antiterrorism Officer (ATO) Level II GS109.16

- FPCON (Normal, A, B, C, D) vs Terrorist Threat Levels (Low, Med, Signif, High) and who sets them
- Exterior Security Lighting PY109.16
- 4 Types (Continuous, Standby, Emergency, Movable)
- Govt Security force vs Contracted Security Force
- 4 Military Working Dog Capabilities (Seek, Detect, Bite and Hold, Guard a Suspect)

Course-Specific Test Bank

Risk Management for DoD Security Programs (GS102) Questions

Lighting, weapons, closed circuit TV, fences, and locking mechanisms are examples of what category of countermeasure?

Procedural

Facilities

Training

Equipment

An asset value should be assigned based on the perspective of the _____.

Asset Manager

Chief of Security

Program Manager

Asset Owner

You are the one who decides what constitutes an acceptable level of risk for an organization's assets.

True

False

Which of the following questions are used to identify an adversary's intent? (Select all that apply)

What are the vulnerabilities to the risk management system?

What are the adversary's goals?

What level of risk are the adversaries likely to accept?

Are the adversaries willing to risk getting caught?

---

5 of 30

After you've completed all other steps, what final chart would you use to summarize and record your information in order to get the total cost for all countermeasures?

Intent Assessment Chart

Collection Capability Assessment Chart

Threat Assessment Summary Chart

Countermeasure Analysis Chart

---

6 of 30

To assist in analyzing threat data, adversaries are typically grouped into all EXCEPT which of the following categories?

Organizations

Companies

Governments

Individuals

---

7 of 30

After completing the vulnerability assessment in the risk management process, the next step is the _____ assessment.

Countermeasures

Cost/benefit

Risk

Asset

After completing the threat assessment step of the risk management process, what step should be completed next?

Asset assessment

Countermeasures determination

Cost/benefit analysis

Vulnerability assessment

Which of the following is NOT a good interview question for determining an adversary's history?

Does the adversary have the weapons or tools for exploiting or attacking an asset?

Has the adversary attacked or exploited assets and personnel before?

Has the adversary been suspected of attacking or exploiting assets?

Might some foreseeable event cause the adversary to attempt an attack in the future?

Which of the following is one of the five categories of assets?

Facilities

Countermeasures

Vulnerabilities

Using the formula R= (I [T x V]) which of the examples below poses the highest risk:

Asset is assessed as 3 (low), threat is assessed as .75 (critical), and the vulnerability is assessed as .74 (high).

Asset is assessed as 13 (medium), threat is assessed as .50 (high), and vulnerability is assessed as .74 (high).

Asset is assessed as 80 (critical), threat is assessed as .24 (low), and vulnerability is assessed as .37 (medium).

----

12 of 30

The risk management process uses four linguistic values: critical, high, medium, and significant. True or false?

True

False

----

13 of 30

Poor perimeter lighting and unsecured doors are examples of a/an _____ vulnerability?

Facility

Operational

Human

Information

----

14 of 30

The formula R=I [T x V] is used for calculating a risk rating. What risk factors do R, I, T, and V represent?

return, impact, threat, vulnerability

risk, impact, threat, vulnerability

risk, importance, threat, vulnerability

return, importance, threat, vulnerability

----

15 of 30

Awareness programs, two person rules, and passwords are examples of what category of countermeasure?

Manpower

Equipment

Planning

Procedural

The time to implement and oversee the countermeasure, the time to prepare for its implementation, and any time required for follow-up and evaluation have no impact when determining the cost of a countermeasure.

True

False

Identify and characterize the specific vulnerabilities that still exist, given the current countermeasures is a step necessary for _____ _____.

risk rating

risk assignment

regression analysis

threat rating

The process in which the costs and benefits of each alternative countermeasure are compared, and the most appropriate alternative is selected, is called _____.

Cost/benefit analysis

Impact/Cost analysis

Threat/cost analysis

Countermeasure/benefit analysis

The degree of difficulty required to exploit a single vulnerability defines what vulnerability criteria?

Quality

Undesirable event

Effectiveness

Quantity

The number of complementary vulnerabilities that can be exploited defines what vulnerability criteria?

Quantity

Effectiveness

Quality

Undesirable event

Your research shows that specific threat category indicates little or no evidence of capability or intent with no history of actual or planned threats against the assets. The linguistic rating you assign to this asset category is _____.

Negligible

Low

Medium

None

When determining an adversary's history, it is a good idea to ask if the adversary has been suspected of attacking or exploiting assets.

True

False

Determining if an adversary has the requisite technology and skills helps to determine the adversary's

_____.

Intent

Capability

History

Vulnerability

One way to describe asset value is:

What is the impact of an undesirable event?

What is the potential for an event to take place?

What is the level of weakness at the site?

What is the capability of a specific threat?

Identifying the ineffective countermeasures is the first step in the regressive analysis process.

True

False

Given the equation (R= I [T x V]), what is the overall risk after your assessment determined that the asset is 75, the threat level is .62, and the vulnerability level is .49?

7

22.8

74.5

13

A threat is any indication, circumstance, or event, while an adversary is an individual, group, organization, or government.

True

False

When following the Risk Management Process, what is the next thing you should do after identifying significant assets?

Measure impacts

Create a risk assessment worksheet

Identify potential undesirable events

Which of the following questions can help guide you when interviewing SMEs about potential undesirable events?

What critical/valuable equipment is located at this site? Why is it critical and valuable?

What undesirable events regarding a particular asset concern the asset owner?

What critical mission activities take place at this site?

Who are the facility personnel, tenants, customers, and visitors? What relationship do they have to the critical mission activities/operations?

Poor tradecraft practices are an example of a/an _____ vulnerability.

Equipment

Information

Operational

Facility

Introduction to Physical Security (PY011.06) Questions

1 of 30
Which of the following is NOT a responsibility of the Information Systems Owner (ISO)?
Coordinate the physical security measures for information systems
Ensure that security considerations are properly and legally incorporated
Develop contingency plans for information systems

2 of 30
Which of the following statements is true of the Department of Defense's Physical Security Program?
It establishes the standards, criteria, and guidelines for determining whether individuals requiring access to classified information are loyal, trustworthy, and reliable.
It **uses active and passive measures to detect, deter, delay, and/or deny unauthorized access to personnel, installations, equipment, facilities, activities, and operation.**
It defines the requirements for safeguarding classified information in the possession of government contractors, licensees, or grantees in the most efficient and cost-effective manner possible.
It promotes the proper and effective classification, protection, and downgrading of official information in the interest of national security.

3 of 30
A _____ is an indication, circumstance, or event with the potential to cause loss or damage of an asset or capability.
Threat
Risk
Vulnerability
Compromise

4 of 30
Interior Intrusion Detection Systems includes proximity detectors, interior barrier protectors, volumetric detectors, and _____.

Interior barrier switches
Volumetric controls
Operable opening switches
Thermal detectors

---

5 of 30
_____ are integral components used to protect the perimeter of a facility or installation.
Key cards
Barrier devices
Locks
Guard staff

---

6 of 30
The _____ is responsible for supporting the physical security mission by managing, implementing, and directing an installation or facility's physical security program.
Counterintelligence Agent
Antiterrorism Officer
Physical Security Officer
Operational Security Officer
Commander or Director

---

7 of 30
Criticality looks at the importance of a part to the whole.
True
False

---

8 of 30
FPCON _____ warrants a routine security posture.
Normal
Alpha
Bravo
Charlie
Delta

---

9 of 30
The two types of intrusion detection systems are _____ and _____.
Secret and Non-Secret
Exterior and Interior

Physical and Virtual
Active and passive

---

10 of 30
An effective counter response to security threats requires _____.
A well-defined line of command
Comprehensive planning
Alternative power sources
Additional budget allocations

---

11 of 30
Lighting plays an important role as part of physical security and countermeasures to protect national security and other DoD assets.
True
False

---

12 of 30
Emergency lighting requires _____ and is used when regular lighting is not available.
Manual Switchover
Escalated Authority
Alternative Power Sources
Additional Staff Resources

---

13 of 30
Government and contract security forces share the same mission to protect national security and other DoD assets.
True
False

---

14 of 30
Interior barrier protectors can be deployed using an _____.
Audio volume controls
Infrared beam and a trip wire
Manual relays
Automatic electronic field and alarm

---

15 of 30

Military Working Dogs help security force members enforce laws and regulations by helping to identify illegal drugs, detect explosives, or _____.
Detect contraband equipment
Prevent physical entry
Prevent theft
Search for individuals

16 of 30
_____ can be used for perimeter security.
Guard stands
Signage
Barbed Wire Fencing
Lights

17 of 30
Security-in-depth is a determination that a facility's security program consists of a combination of layered and complementary security controls.
True
False

18 of 30
Compliance inspections are an effective means to ensure _____ are being met.
Technology reviews
Security feedback reports
Regulatory requirements
Cost effective measures

19 of 30
Point security is a physical security principle that calls for the use of a physical security measure to protect a(n) _____.
Asset with a specific vulnerability level
Specific asset or resource
Specific point of an area requiring protection
Asset with a specific criticality level

20 of 30
When keys are not controlled and something goes missing, the corrective measures can be very costly and time consuming.

True
False

Access control systems can either be _____ or _____ systems.
Passive or active
Manual or remote controlled
Manual or automated electronic
Encrypted or non-encrypted

Weapons or sensitive items such as funds, jewels, or precious metals may be stored in the same security container as classified information.
True
False

Physical Security Officers are responsible for planning, forming, coordinating, and integrating all physical security matters in their installations.
True
False

The _____ approves security containers used to store classified information.
Assigned DoD agency
General Services Administration
Director of National Intelligence
U.S. Environmental Protection Agency

Properly designed facilities provide physical and _____ deterrence to intruders.
Geographic
Criminal
Psychological
Layered

A(n) _____ is an adversary who uses violence or the threat of violence to instill fear, with the intent to coerce or intimidate governments.
Accomplice
Terrorist
Insider
Criminal

---

27 of 30
It is everyone's responsibility within a secure facility to make sure that classified information does not fall into the hands of someone who could cause damage to our national security.
True
False

---

28 of 30
Security-in-depth is a concept that employs _____ security measures.
Layered
Covert
Encrypted
Sequential

---

29 of 30
Which of the following physical security coordinating activities is responsible for conducting criticality, vulnerability, and risk assessments?
Threat Working Group
Antiterrorism Executive Committee
Antiterrorism Working Group

---

30 of 30

There are three major Department of Defense policy documents that govern the Department's Physical Security Program. They are:

(1) DoD Instruction 5200.08, "Security of DoD Installations and Resources and the DoD Physical Security Review Board (PSRB),"

(2) DoD 5200.08-R, "Physical Security Program" Regulation, and

(3) DoDM 5200.01, Volumes 1-4, "DoD Information Security Program."

Which one of these policy documents addresses the physical security aspect of protecting classified information?

DoD 5200.08-R
DoDM 5200.01, Volumes 1-4
DoD Instruction 5200.08

Physical Security Measures (PY103) Questions

1 of 30
What security force functions may be combined?
Static observation posts and access control points
Dispatch control centers and security system monitors
Dispatch control centers and roving patrols
Roving patrols and static observation posts

---

2 of 30
Temporary walls and rigid barriers that establish barriers along approaches within the installation boundary to force vehicles to make tight, slow turns before approaching gates or building entrances are considered active barriers.
True
False

---

3 of 30
Surface lighting is used to display a silhouette of any person passing between the light source and the building or to show the contrast of a person inside the building.
True
False

---

4 of 30
If a raccoon sets off a fence sensor, what kind of alarm occurs?
Nuisance alarm
Intruder alarm
Maintenance alarm
False alarm

---

5 of 30

If nuisance alarms are a continuing problem in an alarm zone, a
_____ may provide the ability to assess alarms before dispatching
security forces.
Premise Control Unit (PCU)
screening equipment system
closed circuit television (CCTV) system
pest detection system (PDS)

6 of 30
An Intrusion Detection System (IDS) used with a closed-circuit television (CCTV) system is
likely to result in distractions to the operator and a reduction in security efficiency.
True
False

7 of 30
What determines and dictates specific procedures that assigned escort personnel must
follow?
Homeland Security Presidential Directive - 12
National Industrial Security Program Operating Manual (NISPOM)
Local directives

8 of 30
Glare projection lighting is used to make it more difficult to see outside a facility from the
inside.
True
False

9 of 30
Using hand-held magnetometers (wands) as back-up for additional screening with fixed
screening equipment is NOT an effective use of this screening equipment.
True
False

10 of 30
What type of Intrusion Detection System (IDS) monitoring provides local centralized
monitoring?
Central station monitoring
Proprietary monitoring

Local monitoring
None of the above

What is the purpose of screening equipment?
To identify potentially dangerous and unauthorized items.
To validate manufacturer-required calibration.
To identify potentially dangerous and unauthorized personnel.
To prevent the unauthorized removal of classified information.

What are the operational phases of an Intrusion Detection system?
Detection, Reporting, Dispatch, and Response/Assessment
Alarm Initiation, Response, Termination, Assessment/Cancellation
Diversion, Response Force Dispatch, Response, Assessment/Cancellation
Alarm Silencing, Dispatch, Response, Termination

What type of access control system requires the user to enter a multi-digit number into a push button or keypad cipher device in order to gain access?
Programmed
Biometric
Automated
Combination
Manual

What are the types of screening equipment most frequently used by the Department of Defense (DoD)?
Intrusive and unobtrusive
Fixed and portable
Portable and closed-circuit television (CCTV)
Detection and reporting

Security forces composed of military personnel and government employees all have the same mission, to protect DoD assets, but security forces composed of contractor personnel have narrower missions.

True
False

A closed circuit television (CCTV) is an especially valuable security asset because it can be used effectively without establishing procedures and providing training in its use.
True
False

Identify a component of Intrusion Detection Systems (IDS)?
Document intrusion
Unauthorized entry
Outdoor usage
Transmission line

Enclaving refers to designating _____ of extreme or high security within a _____ of moderate security.
points ... plain
islands ... sea
elements ... bloc
mountains ... valley

What type of access control system uses verification of an acceptable form of identification such as the Common Access Card, or CAC?
Combination
Automated
Mechanical
Physical
Manual
Biometric

A visitor with a record in the Joint Personnel Adjudication System (JPAS) reflecting the appropriate level of access eligibility but who does not have a verified need-to-know for information protected within the controlled area would require

_____.
an "escort required" visitor badge and escort
an "escort required" visitor badge only
a CAC and escort
a visitor badge

If an electrical surge caused by a thunderstorm activates a sensor, what kind of alarm occurs?
Nuisance alarm
Maintenance alarm
False alarm
Intruder alarm

What type of access control system is a card swipe, with or without a personal identification number, or PIN?
Physical
Combination
Biometric
Automated
Manual

What are the characteristics of passive barrier systems?
Require manual operation by security forces
Have substantial bulk or mass
Have moving parts
Are permanently installed or require heavy equipment to move

The goal of _____ security is to adequately supervise and protect the communications between the alarmed area and the monitoring station to prevent modification and substitution of the transmitted signal.
Premise Control Unit (PCU)
monitoring station, equipment, and personnel
transmission line
sensor and detector

What type of Intrusion Detection System (IDS) monitoring is required if response by local on-site personnel or security is satisfactory?
Local monitoring
Central station monitoring
Proprietary monitoring
None of the above

What Intrusion Detection System (IDS) operational phase is activated when a sensor responds to stimuli?
Reporting
Response/Assessment
Dispatch
Detection

How are military working dogs employed by security force members?
Assist in detecting explosives
Assist in law enforcement
Assist in drug testing
Assist in confrontation management
Assist in pest control

To protect consolidated resources, such as an installation or facility, you would employ
_____ security to provide the best protection.
central
area
over-arching
point

The perimeter barrier of an installation or facility may include the features of the surrounding landscaping.
True
False

The types of site lighting within DoD are_____.
Moveable
Emergency
Continuous
Standby
All the above

Physical Security Planning and Implementation Measures (PY106) Questions

1 of 30

Threat levels assist senior leaders to determine the appropriate _____ level.

FPCON

SOP

Classification designation

GSA security specification

----

2 of 30

_____ issue Force Protections Conditions (FPCONs).

The DHS and COCOMs

COCOMs and installation commanders/facility directors

The DIA and COCOMs

----

3 of 30

Antiterrorism measures used by the DoD to communicate levels of threat in specific areas and what security measures are to be used in response to those threats are called
_____.

THREATCONs and Terrorist Threat Levels

FPCONs and THREATCONs

Terrorist Threat Levels and FPCONs

_____ establish duties, roles, and responsibilities at individual assignments, checkpoints, gates, and guard posts.

Post Orders

Physical Security Plans (PSP)

Memorandums of Understanding (MOU)

_____ are conducted by peers or by senior agency personnel in the chain-of-command.

Staff assist visits

Compliance inspections

Self-inspections

Surveys

Which of the following physical security coordinating activities is made up of multiple individuals such as the Antiterrorism Officer, a Counterintelligence representative, Operations Security officer, and Law Enforcement representative?

Antiterrorism Working Group

Threat Working Group

Antiterrorism Executive Committee

_____ are formal reviews conducted by senior officials to verify policies are being followed, identify weaknesses, promote cost-effectiveness and quality performance, and serve as opportunity for security education.

Self-inspections

Compliance inspections

Staff assist visits

Surveys

----

8 of 30

The inspector's role is only to identify weaknesses and security violations and should not extend to suggesting corrective action.

True

False

----

9 of 30

Antiterrorism physical security measures incorporate detection, deterrence, denial, and _____

Delay

Evaluation

Determination

Notification

----

10 of 30

Conducting a survey is a useful way to determine the physical security posture of an installation or facility.

True

False

Openings that have a cross-section area of _____ or greater, are considered man-passable, and therefore must be eliminated or secured to prevent a person from crawling through them.

36 square inches

96 square inches

128 square inches

----

12 of 30

Although the specific content of a Physical Security Plan may vary between components, installations, units, or activities, the format remains the same.

True

False

----

13 of 30

_____ are measures taken to protect personnel and assets from attack.

Continuity of Operations Plan

DoD Terrorist Threat Levels

Force Protection Conditions

----

14 of 30

_____ are low, moderate, significant, and high.

DoD Terrorist Threat Levels

Force Protection Conditions

Counterterrorism measures

----

15 of 30

A _____ defines emergency delegations of authority and orders of succession to ensure DoD Component Mission Essential Functions (MEFs) continue under all circumstances.

Continuity of Operations Plan (COOP)

Physical Security Plan (PSP)

Memorandum of Agreement (MOA)

----

16 of 30

You must use the _____ process to acquire and analyze the information necessary for protecting assets and allocating security resources against the threats

oversight and inspection

physical security implementation

risk management

----

17 of 30

_____ detail(s) the security measures for a facility or installation.

A Physical Security Plan (PSP)

Post Orders

Standard Operating Procedures (SOP)

----

18 of 30

_____ are weaknesses, characteristics, or circumstances that can be exploited by an adversary to gain access to or information from an asset.

Threats

Risks

Vulnerabilities

----

19 of 30

The _____ develops and refines terrorism threat assessments and coordinates and disseminates threat warnings, reports, and summaries.

Antiterrorism Working Group (ATWG)

Threat Working Group (TWG)

Defense Critical Infrastructure Protection (DCIP) Working Group

----

20 of 30

Every effort should be made to locate lights so they avoid creating a glare problem for both guards and anyone approaching the boundary.

True

False

----

21 of 30

_____ lighting is manually or automatically turned on when suspicious activity is detected or suspected by the security force, alarm system, or motion detector

Standby

Emergency

Continuous

----

22 of 30

_____ is commonly used in combat environments.

Barbed wire

Metal ornamental high security

Concertina wire

----

23 of 30

The Physical Security Plan should cover the assets of any tenant organizations in the installation or facility

True

False

_____ develop and maintain physical security plans.

Operations Security (OPSEC) Officers

Defense Critical Infrastructure Protection (DCIP) Program Officers

Physical Security Officers

_____ is defined as actions taken to prevent or mitigate hostile actions against DoD personnel including family members, resources, facilities, and critical information.

Counterterrorism

Force Protection

Operations Security

Personnel Defense

_____, the inspector should review any local security directives, the facility's Physical Security Plan, its Standard Operating Procedures, and any previous inspection reports, exceptions and waivers.

When preparing the inspection report

During the inspection

In preparing for an inspection

Authorities directing implementation may augment their FPCON by adding security measures from higher FPCON standards as they deem necessary.

True

False

Antiterrorism physical security measures integrate facilities, equipment, personnel, and _____ into a comprehensive effort designed to provide maximum protection to personnel and other DoD assets.

Working Dogs

Reference manuals

Procedures

Associated organizations

In _____, you must consider the cost versus the benefit of protecting DoD assets.

assessing risks

making risk management decisions

identifying vulnerabilities

There is a one for one correlation between Terrorist Threat Levels and Force Protection Conditions.

True

False

Exterior Security Lighting (PY109) Questions

1 of 25
When making a decision on the types of poles or mounts to be used, the overall design configuration of the site must be considered.
True
False

2 of 25
Using light fixtures on the lower parts of buildings and structures may expose an intruder who is relying on darkness for concealment.
True
False

3 of 25
In AA&E storage areas, exterior light switches should only be installed_____.
when necessary to facilitate immediate entry into a structure
on facilities with small explosive quantities
so that they are accessible only to individuals with authorized access
on perimeter light poles

4 of 25
Surface lighting illuminates the face of a building from the_____.
side
top down
ground up

5 of 25
What type of criminal or vandal does security lighting deter?
Unsophisticated
Surreptitious
Sophisticated

6 of 25
Lighting trespass is when color shift causes problems with identifying persons and objects in the lighted area.
True
False

Light trespass could cause interference with security in the adjoining area.
True
False

By reducing glare you increase the vertical illuminance on approaching vehicles or individuals, while increasing visibility for guards and patrols.
True
False

When using controlled lighting on a perimeter, the lamps are positioned to shine

_____.

down and out
horizontally
up and out
directly down

Surface lighting assists the security force by concealing their location.
True
False

Which of the following statements is true?
No more than one luminaire can be mounted on any pole regardless of height.
More than one luminaire can be mounted on taller poles.

Luminance is measured in either watts or light efficacy.
True
False

This luminaire is used to reduce direct glare when lighting medium to large areas, where

control of spill light is important and used primarily in parking lots next to residential areas.
Post top uncontrolled
Low mounted sight lighting
Refractor
Cut-off

14 of 25
Proper illumination may lead a potential intruder to believe detection is inevitable.
True
False

15 of 25
Under what circumstances can the use of direct glare enhance security?
Personnel and vehicle entry/check points
Roadways
Exterior perimeters

16 of 25
With glare projection, guards are concealed in comparative darkness and are able to observe the area.
True
False

17 of 25
A _____ is a device used with an electric discharge light source to obtain the necessary circuit conditions (voltage, current) for starting and operating.
lens
luminaire
ballast
lamp

18 of 25
Security lighting facilitates the detection of unauthorized persons approaching or attempting malicious acts within the area.
True
False

19 of 25
This low to medium wattage luminaire is used when it is necessary to direct most light into the desired area and primarily used in medium to small areas and pedestrian walkways.
Post top controlled
Cut-off
Post top uncontrolled

20 of 25
What lighting system is used during power failures or other situations when normal systems become inoperative?
Standby
Portable
Emergency
Continuous

21 of 25
Fenced perimeters are considered to be _____, _____, or _____.
controlled, semi-controlled, or uncontrolled
controlled, cut-off, or semi-cut-off
isolated, semi-isolated, or non-isolated

22 of 25
_____ refers to how the amount of light degrades over time with the amount of energy consumed remaining constant, while the light output slowly reduces.
Lamp lumen depreciation
Lamp wattage
Lamp efficiency
None of the above

23 of 25
The purpose of security lighting is to_____.
delay the intruder, and respond to assess the situation
discourage attempts at entry by intruders
detect an intrusion, and assess the situation to see what triggered the alarm

24 of 25
The amount of horizontal illuminance is far more important than vertical in many security lighting applications.

True
False

Which of the following types of security lighting systems is the most common?
Emergency
Continuous
Standby
Portable

Lock and Key Systems (PY104) Questions

As a best practice, when a combination is changed, how many times should the new combination by tried before closing the door or drawer?

3
2
1

Which lock is approved under the Federal Specification FF-P-110?
S&G 8077
S&G 2740B
S&G 2937
S&G 2740

Which of the following is an example of a locking device?

Cylinder
Bolt
Key

Which type of lock commonly has a knob or latch on both sides of the door?

Padlocks
Deadbolt locks
Mortise locks

You would like to use the most current built-in combination lock. Which of these locks should you use?

S&G 2740B electromechanical lock
Kaba Mas X-07 electromechanical lock
S&G 8077 padlock

Which of the following is the purpose of a lock's switching device?

To allow or deny entry into a container or area
To keep the area or container secured
To authorize the locking device to open

A Life Safety is an emergency egress hardware, installed to allow exit by pushing on a push bar or panic bar hardware from inside so the door automatically unlocks and swings outward.
True
False

Using birth dates when changing combination numbers is acceptable as long as you don't use your own.
True
False

Which of the following must you do when opening an electromechanical lock such as the X-07, X-08, X-09, and X-10?

Count the number of dial rotations in between each number in the combination.
Turn the dial and stop it when you see the correct number displayed on the LCD.

Mortise locks are _____ the frame of a door and used when a door knob or latch are required for entry.

riveted onto
hung from
recessed into
attached to

You need to review the requirements that electromechanical locks meet. Which of the following specifications should you reference?

Federal Specification FF-L-2740B
Federal Specification FF-P-110
Federal Specification FF-L-2937

Who is responsible for overall protection of keys and spare locks?
Physical Security Specialist
Security Officer
Key Custodian

Which of the following statements about combination locks is true?

A combination lock can only be a padlock.
A combination lock can be a built-in lock or a padlock.
A combination lock can only be a built-in lock.

14 of 30

Which type of cylinder provides a locking solution that minimizes the rekeying burden?

Interchangeable core cylinder
Rim cylinder
Mortise cylinder

15 of 30

A key and lock custodian should change or rotate locks at least _____.

monthly
annually
quarterly

16 of 30

You are using the S&G 8077/AD combination padlock to secure Secret and Confidential information. What may be required?

Nothing else would be required as these can always be used on their own.
NAPEC 0958 or NAPEC 1300 hasps
Supplemental controls

17 of 30

How are electromechanical locks powered?

Electricity-powered
Self-powered and battery-powered
Solar powered

18 of 30

You are making a decision about the locking system to be used in a bulk storage area that contains classified information. Which type of key-operated lock should you use?

A built-in lock

An approved padlock

The use of a master key system is not acceptable in _____.

barracks
general office areas
secure areas

What factor affects decisions made about which users may access a lock, time restrictions on locking/unlocking a lock, and automatic versus manual relocking of a lock?
Life safety
The cost of a lock
The level of security needed

What operates most key-operated locks?

Cylinders
Triggers
Wheel packs

Which dial rotation do the X-09 and X-10 electromechanical built-in combination locks have in common?

right only
left only
left-right-left

Which type of cylinder is most commonly used on inward-opening or front doors?

Interchangeable core cylinder
Mortise cylinder
Rim cylinder

---

24 of 30

Which statement <u>best</u> describes the relationship between a locking solution's level of protection and its cost and labor effort?

Locking solutions that provide a higher level of protection are more costly, but less labor-intensive.
Locking solutions do not have a correlation between level of protection and cost and labor effort; it simply depends on the specific solution.
Locking solutions that provide a higher level of protection are more costly and labor-intensive.

---

25 of 30

S&G 833C and 951 locks are _____.

low security padlocks
medium security padlocks
high security padlocks

---

26 of 30

An advantage of a master key system is that _____.

master keys are more difficult to pick
it is convenient for the owner or manager of the locking system
master keys are easier to replace if lost

---

27 of 30

Which of the following should you do before changing a combination?

Try the combination three times
Call your FSO
Lock drawer in open position

Susan Johnson knows the combination to a security container and Susan lost her clearance today, but she was not terminated from her job. What must happen?

The combination on that security container must be changed.
Nothing must happen. Susan knows she's no longer authorized and will not access the storage container.
The security container must be replaced.

When assessing the life safety aspect of a locking solution for a facility door, which of the following must be considered?

The door must be locked to prevent unauthorized entry and exit.
The door must be locked to prevent unauthorized entry, but allow those inside to exit through the door without unlocking it.
The door must be unlocked so that those inside can exit without having to unlock the door.

The type of locking device required is determined by the environment and _____.
Facility classification
Asset type
Installation commander
Authorized personnel

PSC General Knowledge Test Bank

List three policies or regulations that govern the DoD physical security program.

DoD 5200.08-Regulation Physical Security Program
DoD Manual 5100.76 Physical Security of Sensitive Conventional Arms, Ammunition, and Explosives (AA&E)
DoD Manual 5105.21 Sensitive Compartmented Information (SCI) Administrative Security Manual: Administration of Physical Security, Visitor Control, and Technical Security

Describe the purpose of the DoD 5200.08-R, Physical Security Program.

The regulation implements DoD policies and provides minimum standards for the physical protection of DoD personnel, installations, operations, and related resources.

Source: DoD 5200.08-R, Physical Security Program

Briefly describe Security-in-Depth.

A determination by the senior agency official that a facility's security program consists of layered and complimentary security controls sufficient to deter, detect, and document unauthorized entry and movement within the facility.

Source: DoD 5200.08-R, Physical Security Program, DL1.17

List three examples of Security-in-Depth.

Perimeter fence
Employee/visitor access control
Intrusion detection system
Random guard patrols
Closed circuit video monitoring

Source: DoD 5200.08-R, Physical Security Program

DoD 5200.01, Volume 3, DoD Information Security Program: Protection of Classified Information (Glossary)

List three examples of physical security threats.

Foreign intelligence services
Foreign military and paramilitary forces
Terrorists
Saboteurs
Criminals
Protest groups
Disaffected persons
Natural disasters

Source: DoD 5200.08-R, Change 1, Physical Security Program, paragraphs C2.1.2 and C3.4, EMERGENCY PLANNING

(See also DTM 08-004 and DTM 09-012.)

List five of the nine capabilities a security system must provide to achieve Security-in-Depth.

Deter
Detect
Identify
Track
Assess
Record
Communicate
Delay
Respond

Source: DoD 5200.08-R, Change 1, Physical Security Program, paragraph C.2.3.1

DoD 5200.01, Volume 3, DoD Information Security Program: Protection of Classified Information (Glossary)

DTM 09-012, Change 4, April 22, 2014, Interim Policy Guidance for DoD Physical Access Control

Briefly describe the elements of a restricted area.

An area (land, sea, or air) in which there are special restrictive measures employed to prevent or minimize incursions and/or interference, or where special security measures are employed to prevent unauthorized entry. Restricted areas must be authorized by the installation/activity commander/director, properly posted, and employ physical security measures.

Source: DoD 5200.08-R, Physical Security Program, DL1.12

What are some of the considerations a physical security professional should take into account for controlling access?

Escort qualifications, responsibilities, and authorizations

Sponsorship qualifications, responsibilities, and authorizations
Access privileges at each security level and each FPCON
Mission-essential employee designation, if applicable
Emergency response designation, if applicable
Day and time designation for access
Locations authorized for access

Source: DTM 09-012, December 8, 2009, Interim Policy Guidance for DoD Physical Access Control (p. 12)

What must occur for an individual to be provided access without an escort?

The individual must have been identity proofed and favorably vetted in accordance with applicable regulations.

Source: DTM 09-012, December 8, 2009, Interim Policy Guidance for DoD Physical Access Control (p. 21)

At minimum, what should inspections of Arms, Ammunition, and Explosives (AA&E) storage facilities include?

Review physical security measures and policy compliance
Review existing deviations from policy
Review suitability and screening of personnel with access to AA&E
Review inventory and accountability procedures
Facility design and construction

Source: DODM 5100.76, Physical Security of Sensitive Conventional Arms, Ammunition and Explosives (AA&E), paragraph 4: Inspections and Audits

Which federal specification defines the manufacturing requirements for armory vault doors and security vault doors?

Federal Specification AA-D-600D, Door, Vault, Security.

Source: Federal Specification AA-D-600D, Door, Vault, Security

What is the central and overriding objective for nuclear security?

The denial of unauthorized access, as outlined in National Security Presidential Directive-28.

Source: DODI O-5210.63, DODI DoD Procedures, Nuclear Reactors-Material

DODD 5210.41, Security Policy for Protecting Nuclear Weapons

What factors do DoD Components consider when determining security priority for weapons systems platforms?

Mission
Location and vulnerability
Operational readiness
Value
Classification
Replacement costs

Source: DoD 5200.08-R, Physical Security Program, C4.2.2

Who must approve all Intrusion Detection Equipment (IDE) installed on Open Storage Areas?

DoD Components approve Underwriters Laboratories' listed equipment.

Source: DODM 5200.01, Volume 3, Change 2, DoD Information Security Program: Protection of Classified Information

Note. Acceptability of Equipment: All IDE must be Underwriters Laboratories (UL)-listed or equivalent and approved by the DoD Component (p. 47, paragraph c).

What reference governs the Certification and Accreditation (C&A) for storage of DoD collateral Classified Information Systems?

DODM 5200.01, DoD Information Security Program, Volume 3, Protection of Classified Information.

Source: DODM 5200.01, Volume 3, Change 2, DoD Information Security Program: Protection of Classified Information

Note. If material is SCI, then DODM 5105.21 Volume 2, Sensitive Compartmented Information (SCI) Administrative Security Manual: Administration of Physical Security, Visitor Control, and Technical Security applies.

To whom should incidents involving stolen, lost, or recovered Arms, Ammunition, and Explosives (AA&E), which cause significant news coverage or have the potential to cause such coverage, be reported?

The Office of the Under Secretary of Defense for Intelligence.

Source: DODM 5100.76, Physical Security of Sensitive Conventional Arms, Ammunition, and Explosives, Enclosure 11

What are included as considerations during inspections of Arms, Ammunition, and Explosives (AA&E) storage facilities?

Review of physical security measures and policy compliance
Review of existing deviations from policy
Review of suitability and screening of personnel with access to AA&E
Inventory and accountability procedures
Facility design and construction

Source: DODM 5100.76-M, Physical Security of Sensitive Conventional Arms, Ammunition, and Explosives, April 17, 2012 (p. 16)

Who is responsible for issuing instructions governing the security of weapons systems within their inventory?

Each DoD Component head.

Source: DoD 5200.08-R, Physical Security Program, April 9, 2007 (p. 20)

What are the four considerations/risk factors used for determining the security risk category (SRC) of sensitive conventional Arms, Ammunition, and Explosives (AA&E)?

Utility
Casualty or damage risk

Adaptability risk
Portability risk

Source: DODM 5100.76-M, Physical Security of Sensitive Conventional Arms, Ammunition, and Explosives, April 17, 2012 (pp. 44-45)

What is the purpose of intrusion detection systems?

To detect unauthorized penetration into a secured area.

Source: DODM 5200.01, Volume 3, DoD Information Security Program: Protection of Classified Information, Enclosure 3, paragraph 2a

UFC 4-021-02, Electronic Security Systems

Describe the three types of lighting systems used for security lighting.

Continuous lighting: A series of fixed lights arranged to continuously illuminate a given area.
Standby lighting: Luminaires are either automatically or manually turned on at times when suspicious activity is detected by security personnel or an intrusion detection system. A standby system creates the impression of activity and may offer a deterrent value while also conserving energy.
Moveable lighting: Manually-operated searchlights that may be lighted during hours of darkness or as needed, and is normally used to supplement continuous or standby lighting.

Source: UFC 3-530-01, Exterior Lighting (pp. 69-70)

What is the reference that provides minimum construction requirements for fencing?

UFC 4-022-03, Security Fences and Gates.

Source: UFC 4-022-03, Security Fences and Gates, Chapter 2, paragraphs 2-2.1 and 2-2.1.1

List the types of buildings that are exempt from certain DoD antiterrorism site design standards.

Low occupancy buildings
Low occupancy family housing
Fisher houses

Town centers

Enhanced use leases

Transitional structures and spaces

Temporary and re-locatable buildings

Construction administration structures

Recruiting stations in leased spaces

Stand-alone gas stations and car care centers

Military protective construction (designed to NATO or equivalent standards)

Stand-alone franchised fast food operations

Stand-alone shoppettes, minimarts, and similarly-sized commissaries

Small stand-alone commercial, bank, and pharmacy facilities

Source: UFC 4-010-01, DoD Minimum Antiterrorism Standards for Buildings (pp. 13-15)

Name examples of authorized locking devices used within the Department of Defense.

Cylindrical locksets

Dead-bolt locksets

Drop-bolt locks

Padlocks

Mechanical push-button combination locks

Mechanical combination locks

Electro-mechanical combination locks

Warded locks

Pin tumbler locks

Source: Note. Refer to the DoD Lock Program, which prescribes authorized locks for specific assets.

http://www.navfac.navy.mil/navfac_worldwide/specialty_centers/exwc/products_and_services/capital_improvements/dod_lock/Training/LockProgramTraining.html

Which types of locks are associated with Federal Specification FF-L-2740 and are approved for storage of all types of classified materials, regardless of classification?

Electromechanical combination locks, which include the X-07, X-08, X-09, and S&G 2740, for classified material stored in security containers.

Source: Federal Specification FF-L-2740: Locks, Combination

Explain strengths and weaknesses of various types of padlocks.

Low security padlocks (also known as secondary padlocks) are used for deterrence purposes but provide minimal resistance to force.

High security padlocks deploy a high security hasp, provide maximum resistance to unauthorized entry, and may be used to secure arms, ammunition, and explosives facilities.

Source: Note. Refer to the DoD Lock Program, which prescribes authorized locks for specific assets.

http://www.navfac.navy.mil/navfac_worldwide/specialty_centers/exwc/products_and_services/capital_improvements/dod_lock/Training/LockProgramTraining.html

What are some of the primary uses of fencing?

Provides a legal boundary by defining the outermost limit of a facility
Assists in controlling and screening authorized vehicle entries into a secured area by deterring overt entry elsewhere along the boundary
Supports detection, assessment, and other security functions by providing a "clear zone" for installing lighting, intrusion detection equipment, and CCTV
Deters "casual" intruders from penetrating into a secured area by presenting a barrier that requires over action to penetrate
Causes an intruder to make an overt action that will demonstrate intent

Source: UFC 4-022-02, Selection and Application of Vehicle Barriers, June 8, 2009, Change 1, August 9, 2010 (p. 30)

What are some examples of passive barrier systems?

Concrete-filled bollard
Concrete median (also known as Jersey barrier)
King Tut block
Concrete planter
Excavations and ditches
Guardrails
Heavy equipment tires
Tire shredders
Steel cable barriers
Steel cable-reinforced chain link fencing

Reinforced concrete knee walls

Source: UFC 4-022-02, Selection and Application of Vehicle Barriers, June 8, 2009, Change 1, August 9, 2010 (pp. 52-73)

What is the purpose of deploying glare projection?

Glare projection makes it difficult for potential intruders to see inside the area being protected.

Source: UFC 3-530-01, Interior and Exterior Lighting Systems and Controls, August 22, 2006, including Change 3, September 1, 2013 (p. 105)

Define the two main types of electromechanical locks according to Federal Specification FF-L-2740B.

Basic Self-Contained: Does not have external power source, external data transfer port, or ability to transfer data

Interoperable/Networked: Power source may be contained within and integral to lock assembly; power source may be replaceable; external data transfers shall meet Federal Information Processing Standards (FIPS); data transfers may be used to monitor authorized/unauthorized openings, personnel access, combination verification, and combination changes

Source: FF-L-2740B, Federal Specification Locks, Combination, Electromechanical, June 15, 2011 (p. 1)

The DoD Antiterrorism Standards are applicable to which types of buildings?

New construction
Existing buildings
Major investments
Change of occupancy level
Window replacement
Roadway improvement projects
Building additions
Leased buildings
Partial occupancy
National Guard buildings
Visitor centers and museums
Expeditionary structures

Source: UFC 4-010-01, DoD Minimum Antiterrorism Standards for Buildings, February 9, 2012 (pp. 9-13)

What are some of the exemptions to the DoD Antiterrorism Standards?

Low occupancy buildings
Low occupancy family housing
Fisher houses
Town centers
Enhanced use leases
Transitional structures and spaces
Temporary and re-locatable buildings
Construction administration structures
Recruiting stations in leased spaces
Stand-alone gas stations and car care centers
Military protective construction (designed to NATO or equivalent standards)
Stand-alone franchised fast food operations
Stand-alone shopettes, minimarts, and similarly-sized commissaries
Small stand-alone commercial, bank, and pharmacy facilities

Source: UFC 4-010-01, DoD Minimum Antiterrorism Standards for Buildings, February 9, 2012 (pp. 13-15)

What are the four basic functional elements that must operate in an integrated and timely manner to achieve an overall effective security system that defeats design threats?

Intrusion detection and access control sensors and/or guards
Threat assessment from guards and/or Closed-circuit television (CCTV)
Appropriately designed and located barriers
Responding guards

Source: MIL-HDBK-1013/1A, Design Guidelines for Physical Security, December 15, 1993 (pp. 22-23)

What are some of the considerations for selecting and implementing a particular intrusion detection system?

Completeness of coverage
False and nuisance response rates
Probability of detection
Zone at which the alarm occurred

Source: MIL-HDBK-1013/1A, Design Guidelines for Physical Security, December 15, 1993 (p.75)

List two reasons for which physical security programs should be tailored to local conditions.

In overseas areas, COCOMS may deviate from DoD policy where required by treaties, agreements, and arrangements with foreign governments and allied forces.

Threats, vulnerabilities, and critical assets may vary.

Source: DoD 5200.08-R, Physical Security Program, C1.2.1

DODI 2000.12, Antiterrorism Program, paragraph 20 m. (1)

Before loss of Arms, Ammunition, and Explosives (AA&E) can be attributed to any inventory or accountability discrepancy, one must first determine the loss was not a result of what three factors?

Theft
Abandonment
Misappropriation

Source: DODM 5100.76, Physical Security of Sensitive Conventional Arms, Ammunition, and Explosives, paragraph 6

Define the term "risk" within the context of risks, threats, and vulnerabilities.

A measure of consequence of peril, hazard, or loss, which is incurred from a capable aggressor or the environment.

Source: DoD 5200.08-R, Physical Security Program, DL1.13

When planning and/or responding to an emergency, with whom should coordination occur?

Depending on the situation, emergency planning and emergency response may require coordination with local, state, federal, and/or host country officials and organizations.

Source: DoD 5200.08-R, Physical Security Program, C3.4.2.2

See also Dodi 6055.17, Installation Emergency Management Program.

What are the three goals of the DoD Installation Emergency Management Program?

Prepare DoD installations for emergencies
Respond appropriately to protect personnel and save lives
Recover and restore operations after an emergency

Source: DoD 6055.17, Installation Emergency Management Program

What is the role of the National Response Framework (NRF) for installation emergency management?

The NRF establishes clear objectives for a concerted national effort to prevent, prepare for, respond to, and recover from terrorist attacks, major disasters, and other domestic emergencies. The NRF provides the structure and mechanism for a consistent, nationwide approach for federal, state, and local governments to effectively and efficiently work together to manage domestic incidents, regardless of cause, size, or complexity.

Source: DoDI 6055.17, Installation Emergency Management Program, January 13, 2009, Change 1, November 19, 2010 (p. 26)

Define preparedness in the context of emergency management.

Preparedness is the range of deliberate, critical tasks and activities necessary to build, sustain, and improve the operational capability to prevent, protect against, respond to, and recover from domestic incidents. Preparedness is a continuous process.

Preparedness involves efforts at all levels of government and coordination among government, private sector, and non-governmental organizations to identify threats, determine vulnerabilities, and identify required resources. Within the National Incident Management System, preparedness is operationally focused on establishing guidelines, protocols, and standards for planning, training and exercises, personnel qualification and certification, equipment certification, and publication management.

Source: DoDI 6055.17, Installation Emergency Management Program, January 13, 2009, Change 1, November 19, 2010 (p. 48)

The two primary purposes of physical security are protection and _____?
Prevention

A guard checking IDs at the gate of an installation is a good example of what type of security?
Point security

_____ is the layering of physical security countermeasures such as fencing, guards, cameras, lighting, and locks.
Security-in-depth

Before you can conduct a risk analysis, based on the impact and likelihood of an unwanted event happening, what steps in the risk management process must you take first?
Identify assets
Identify threats
Identify vulnerabilities

Which policy guidance would you consult to find the minimum standards for the physical protection of DoD assets?
DoD 5200.08-R, Physical Security Program

Which policy should you consult to find the physical security requirements of protecting classified information?
DoDM 5200.01, Volumes 1-4 DoD Information Security Program

Which policy authorizes commanders to issue regulations for the protection or security of property and places under their command?
DoDI 5200.08, Security of DoD Installations and Resources and the DoD Physical Security Review Board (PSRB)

Who is charged with management, implementation, and direction of all physical security programs?
Physical Security Officer

Who is responsible for providing valuable information on the capabilities, intentions, and threats of adversaries?
CI Support

Who is responsible for developing countermeasures against potential threats to national security and other DoD assets?
OPSEC Officer

Which of the following individuals should be included in a Threat Working Group?
Chemical, biological, radiological, nuclear and high yield explosive representative, Information operations representative, Operations security officer, Law enforcement, Counterintelligence, Antiterrorism Officer

Which of these can be made of solid steel to make them more attack resistant?
Doors

Which of these house ventilation systems that should be secured with steel bars?
Roofs

Which of these should be covered with a protective film to make them less dangerous in an attack?
Windows

Which of the following locks are approved to secure classified information or material?
Kaba Mas X-10, S&G 8077/AD

Standby lighting is used when regular lighting is not available?
False

Site lighting is used to enable guard force personnel to observe activities inside or outside the installation?
True

Movable lighting is used when supplemental lighting is needed such as at construction sites?
True

At a minimum _____ should include special and general guard orders, access and material control, protective barriers, lighting systems, locks, and Intrusion Detection Systems (IDS).
Physical Security Plans

_____ establish duties, roles, and responsibilities at individual assignments, checkpoints, gates, and guard posts.
Post Orders

_____provide supplemental guidance for physical security programs and establish procedures for emergency events as well as operational and administrative procedures.
Standard Operating Procedures

True or False. Commanders may only implement measures according to the FPCON level in force at the time.
False

True or False. Commanders must comply with and integrate DoD physical security and installation access control policies into their FPCON plans.
True

True or False. Commanders educate their personnel on the insider threat to DoD elements and personnel.
True

Which of the following statements are true of physical security planning and implementation?
The risk management process must be used to plan which physical security measures should be utilized to protect DoD assets.

Of the following (TERRORIST, FENCE, OPEN UNATTENDED INSTALLATION GATE, ARMS AND AMMUNITION, LOSS OF LIFE) which would best be described as a DoD asset?
ARMS AND AMMUNITION

Which of the following would best be described as a threat? (TERRORIST, FENCE, OPEN UNATTENDED INSTALLATION GATE, ARMS AND AMMUNITION, LOSS OF LIFE)
TERRORIST

Which of the following would best be described as a vulnerability? (TERRORIST, FENCE, OPEN UNATTENDED INSTALLATION GATE, ARMS AND AMMUNITION, LOSS OF LIFE)
OPEN UNATTENDED INSTALLATION GATE

Which of the following would best be described as a risk? (TERRORIST, FENCE, OPEN UNATTENDED INSTALLATION GATE, ARMS AND AMMUNITION, LOSS OF LIFE)
LOSS OF LIFE

Which of the following would best be described as a countermeasure? (TERRORIST, FENCE, OPEN UNATTENDED INSTALLATION GATE, ARMS AND AMMUNITION, LOSS OF LIFE)
FENCE

The _____ is responsible for the installation's antiterrorism program.
Antiterrorism Officer.

_____ is responsible for providing valuable information on the capabilities, intentions, and threats of adversaries.
CI Support

The _____ analyzes threats to assets and their vulnerabilities
OPSEC Officer

_____ must be included in the intelligence gathering process so that they can be part of coordinating emergency responses and criminal incidents on a Federal installation.
Law Enforcement

The _____ is charged with the management, implementation, and direction of all physical security programs.
Physical Security Officer

The _____ is responsible for the safety of people and property under their command.
Installation Commander/ Facility Director.

The _____ is responsible for mitigating risks against Defense Critical Infrastructure assets that support the mission of an installation or facility.
DCIP Officer

Flashlights are a reliable form of continuous lighting (TRUE OR FALSE)
FALSE

Emergency lighting depends upon the power supply of the utility company (TRUE OR FALSE)
FALSE

Standby lighting is the type of lighting used when the primary power source fails. (TRUE OR FALSE)
FALSE

Certain types of lighting can incapacitate an intruder. (TRUE OR FALSE)

TRUE

Controlled lighting is used to illuminate the perimeter of a facility. (TRUE OR FALSE)
TRUE

_____ is often used as a temporary barrier when rolled out on the ground.
Concertina wire.

_____ can be used as permanent standalone fencing but is more often used as an outrigger on the top of the chain link fencing.
Barbed wire.

_____ is more difficult for intruders to scale.
Metal ornamental high-security fencing.

_____ is a common type of perimeter fencing for DoD facilities.
Chain-link fencing.

CCTV can deter loss, theft, or misuse of government property and resources. (TRUE OR FALSE)
TRUE

Access control systems help to prevent unauthorized entry. (TRUE OR FALSE)
TRUE

Cost and risk must always be considered when planning which physical security measures to use in a facility or installation. (TRUE OR FALSE)
TRUE

Securing man-passable openings is one of the most overlooked physical security protective measures. (TRUE OR FALSE)
TRUE

Provisions for one entity, such as a DoD activity or local law enforcement, fire, and medical services, to provide security assistance to another entity IS_____
MOA/MOU (MEMORANDUM OF UNDERSTANDING (AGREEMENT)

There are five FPCONs for DoD. Name them.
NORMAL, ALPHA, BRAVO, CHARLIE, AND DELTA

_____applies when a general global threat of possible terrorist activity exists and warrants a routine security posture.
NORMAL

_____applies when there is an increased general threat of possible terrorist activity against personnel or facilities, the nature and extent of which are unpredictable.
ALPHA

_____applies when an increased or more predictable threat of terrorist activity exists.

BRAVO

_____applies when an incident occurs or intelligence is received indicating some form of terrorist action or targeting against personnel or facilities is likely.
CHARLIE

_____applies in the immediate area where a terrorist attack has occurred or when intelligence has been received that terrorist action against a specific location or person is imminent.
DELTA

Who issue FPCONs?
DIA

System that standardizes the identification and recommended preventive actions and responses to terrorist threats against U.S. assets is
FORCE PROTECTION CONDITIONS

Most common and informal oversight tool; immediate action taken to correct deficiencies.
DAY TO DAY OBSERVATIONS

Integrating layers of security to protect DoD assets
SECURITY IN DEPTH

Barbed wire and concertina wire may serve as a protective barrier by simply uncoiling it and laying it on the ground. (TRUE OR FALSE)
TRUE

Jersey barriers may be placed around buildings to prevent vehicles from getting too close to the buildings. (TRUE OR FALSE)
TRUE

Barbed wire is also known as razor wire. (TRUE OR FALSE)
FALSE

This method is intended to display a silhouette of any person passing between the light source and the building or to show the contrast of a person inside the building.
SURFACE LIGHTING

This method is intended to make the inside of a protected area difficult to see from outside the protected area.
GLARE PROJECTION

This method is intended to limit the width of the lighted strip outside the perimeter of a protected area so as not to interfere with adjoining property, nearby highways, railroads, navigable waters, or airports.
CONTROLLED LIGHTING

Contract security forces may be either military or civilian. (TRUE OR FALSE)
FALSE

Internal reviews conducted by members of the organization to aid internal control and ensure cost-effective security program is _____.
Management/self-inspections

Formal reviews conducted by senior officials in the chain-of-command is_____
Compliance inspections

Validate baseline security posture when personnel assume security responsibilities or as a prelude to a formal inspection is_____
Staff assist visits

Can be self-initiated or directed by higher authorities to determine the physical security posture of an installation or facility is _____.
Surveys

Most common and informal oversight tool; immediate action taken to correct deficiencies.
Day-to-day observations

Risk management is a five-step process that provides a framework for collecting and evaluating information. Name the 5-step   risk management process.
1. Assess assets (identify value of asset and degree of impact if asset is damaged or lost)
2. Assess threats (type and degree of threat)
3. Assess vulnerabilities (identification and extent of vulnerabilities)
4. Assess risks (calculation of risks)
5. Determine countermeasures (security countermeasure options that can reduce or mitigate risks cost effectively

Assets fall into 5 categories, name all 5 of them.
1. People
2. Information
3. Equipment
4. Facilities and
5. Activities and Operations

Who provides construction and security requirements for SCIFs?
Director of National Intelligence (DNI)

Who provides accreditation for SCIFs?
Defense Intelligence Agency (DIA)

They are used by the intelligence community to store classified information. _____
SCIFs are used by the intelligence community to store classified information called Sensitive Compartmented Information (SCI).

Warning signs must be posted at each boundary of a restricted area and must be conspicuous to those approaching on foot or by vehicle. True or False
True

The use of master key systems is acceptable in the storage of AA&E.
False. The use of master key systems is not authorized in AA&E storage facilities.

Integrating layers of security to protect DoD assets is_____
Security-In-Depth

Guarding a specific asset or resource_____
Point Security

Protecting an entire area such as an installation or facility is _____
Area Security

Designating islands of high security within a sea of moderate security is _____
Enclaving

The first line of defense in any physical security system is usually some form of _____
perimeter protection system

What kind of fencing is used when a stationary perimeter requires protection?
Permanent

What kind of fencing can be used as a temporary perimeter to establish psychological barriers and to channel pedestrian and vehicle movement?
Temporary

There are four types of site lighting used by DoD installations and facilities. They are?
continuous, standby, emergency, and movable

This method is intended to display a silhouette of any person passing between the light source and the building or to show the contrast of a person inside the building.
Surface Lighting

This method is intended to make the inside of a protected area difficult to see from outside the protected area.
Glare Projection

This method is intended to limit the width of the lighted strip outside the perimeter of a protected area so as not to interfere with adjoining property, nearby highways, railroads, navigable waters, or airports.
Controlled Lighting

The basic manual access control system is simply_____
personal recognition.

Lock and key systems are _____, _____, or_____ used on doors or containers to restrict access to the area or property enclosed.
mechanical, electronic, or electromechanical devices

The primary advantage of a master key system is?
the convenience to its owner or manager

Although there are many different types of locks, they all share three components. They are the locking device, the switching device, and the operating mechanism

Some key-operated locks are built into the door or container they are securing. These are also known as mortise locks, because their case is recessed, or mortised into a door or container.

The _____ is the most common of all door locks in use today.
cylindrical lock

You need to decide what type of locking system to use for a storage closet. The closet does not hold classified or sensitive information, but you want to deter entry. Which type of key-operated lock should you use?
A built-in lock

You are making a decision about the locking system to be used in an area that stores bulk Confidential or Secret material. Which type of key-operated lock should you use?
A padlock

The area you are securing contains conventional arms, ammunition, and explosives (AA&E). Which type of key-operated lock should you use?
A medium security padlock

_____ locks are used for securing classified information.
Electromechanical combination locks are used for securing classified information.

The _____ is the only approved mechanical combination lock under Federal Specification FF-L-2937, used for storage of secret and confidential information under field conditions and in military platforms, AA&E, and other sensitive DoD assets.
S&G 2937 is the only approved mechanical combination lock

When a container is taken out of service, the combination must be reset back to the factory settings. The factory setting for a built-in container lock is_____.
The factory setting for a built-in container lock is 50-25-50.

You are selecting combination locks for your facility and must consider the requirements and features of various combination locks. You need to review the requirements that electromechanical locks meet. Which one should you reference?
Federal Specification FF-L-2740 series

You just received a security container that has the S&G 2740 Electromechanical Safe Lock with a factory setting of 50-25-50. What should you do first?
Calibrate the lock

What are 6 steps of Risk Management Process?

Assess Assets, Assess Threats, Assess Vulnerabilities, Assess Risks, Determine Countermeasures Options, Make Risk Management Decisions

What groups are involved in physical Security planning and implementation?
Antiterrorism Working Group (ATWG), Information Systems Security Managers (ISSMs), Legal Officers, Threat Working Group (TWG), and Defense Critical Infrastructure Working Group (DCIP)

What are barriers?
Used to define boundaries and channel traffic through designated access control points where pedestrians, vessels, and vehicles can be monitored and searched for prohibited items.

Active barriers
Manually or electronically operated gates or turnstiles and hydraulic pop-up vehicle barriers.

Passive barriers
Rely on bulk or mass to be effective and they have no moving parts. (Ex. Vehicle barrier, temporary barrier, etc.)

What type of fencing does DoD use?
Chain link fence constructed of 9-gauge or heavier galvanized steel mesh wore of no more than 2 inches in diameter, be at least 6-8 feet tall with bottom no more than 2 inches off ground.

Metal ornamental high security fencing (with anti-climb inserts, anti-ram cabling, and K-crated crash barrier.

4 types of lighting DoD uses on its installations
Continuous
Standby
Emergency
Moveable

Purpose of lighting
Deters unauthorized entry
Allows security forces to detect intruders before they reach targets
Glare lighting can incapacitate intruders

Planning considerations for lighting
Cost of lights
Characteristics of lights
Positioning of lights
Maintenance

Natural barriers
Topographical features that assist in impeding or denying access to an area. Ex. River, cliff, etc.

Man-passable Opening
96 square inches or greater (ex. Drain pipes, sewers, fire escapes, manhole covers, etc.)

What are advantages of CCTV?
Deters loss, theft, or misuse of government property and resources, as well as unauthorized entry.

Purpose of an Intrusion Detection System
Deter, detect, and document intrusion

What are some factors to consider when selecting IDS?
Asset criticality
Design considerations
Environmental considerations
Location considerations
Perceived threat factor

Considerations for use of CCTV as physical Security measure
Cost of system vs benefit it provides
Color vs black & white
Protection from tampering especially outdoors
Sufficient lighting available

Examples of manual access control systems
Personal recognition
Cipher locks
Acceptable form of ID (ex. Common Access Card)
Joint Personnel Adjudication System (JPAS) Badge ID

Examples of electronically automated access control systems
Biometrics
Swipe card readers
Proximity card systems
Key systems

What are concerns with badge systems?
Mass reissuances of badges cost $
Holder's failure to report loss to appropriate authority
Require more security personnel than manual systems

Parts of Physical Security Plan?
Purpose
Applicability/Area Security
Access and Movement
Security Aids
Annexes

Tactical Environment Considerations for Physical Security Plan
METT-TC (Mission, Enemy, Terrain & Weather, Troops, Time Available, and Civil Considerations)

What are other Physical Security Planning Documents?
Standard Operating Procedures (SOPs)

Post Orders
Continuity of Operations Plan
Memorandum of Agreements and Understanding

Purpose of DoD Antiterrorism Program
Collective, proactive effort focused on prevention and detection of terrorist attacks against DoD personnel, their families, facilities, installations, and infrastructure critical to DoD mission accomplishment.

What are AT tools DoD uses to safeguard DoD assets
DoD Threat Levels
Force Protection Conditions (FPCONs)

What are 4 terror threat levels?
Low, moderate, significant, and high

What organization sets DoD Terror Threat Level identifying potential risk to DoD interests in particular country, regardless of whether US personnel are present?
DIA

True or False: COCOMs can set terror threat levels for specific personnel, family members, units, and installations in countries within their area of responsibility
True

Low threat level
No terror group is detected or low risk of terrorist attack

Moderate threat level
Signifies terrorists are present, no indications of terrorist activity and Operating Environment favors host nation or US

Significant threat level
Terrorists are present and attacking personnel is their preferred method of operation, or that a terrorist group uses large casualty producing attacks as their preferred method, but has limiting operational activity. Operating Environment is neutral.

High terrorist threat level
Terrorists are operationally active and use large casualty-producing attacks as preferred method of operation. Substantial DoD presence, and the Operating Environment favors the terrorist.

What is force protection?
Actions taken to prevent or mitigate hostile actions against DoD assets—including DoD personnel, family members, resources, facilities, and critical information

What are five FPCONs?
FPCON Normal
FPCON Alpha
FPCON Bravo

FPCON Charlie
FPCON Delta

FPCON Normal
A general global threat of possible terrorist activity exists and warrants a routine security posture.

FPCON Alpha
Increased general threat of possible terrorist activity

FPCON Bravo
Increased or more predictable threat of terrorist activity exists

FPCON Charlie
An incident occurs or intelligence is received indicating some form of terrorist action or targeting against personnel or facilities is likely.

FPCON Delta
Applies in the immediate area where a terrorist attack has occurred or when intelligence is received that terrorist action against a specific location or person is imminent.

Purpose of Oversight
Ensure security program complies with DoD and other policies, that the program is cost-effective, and the program is effective in protecting DoD assets against threats such as unauthorized disclosure, misuse, damage, or loss.

Examples of oversight tools
Day-to-day observations
Surveys
Staff-Assisted Visits
Inspections
Reports

DoD Policy that guides DoD Physical Security planning and implementation
DoD 5200.08-R, Physical Security Program
DoDI 5200.08, Security of DoD Installations and Resources and the DoD Physical Security Review Board
DoDD 3020.26, DoD Defense Continuity Program
DoDI 2000.12, DoD Antiterrorism Program
DoDI 2000.16, DoD Antiterrorism Standards
DoD Antiterrorism Officer Guide
DoDM 5200.01, DoD Information Security Program

Objectives of Physical Security: -
Identify Assets
Identify Threats
Identify Vulnerabilities

Primary purpose of Physical Security: -
Prevention - Deter intruders, prevent theft/damage/unauthorized access

Protection - Safeguard against threats

Security-in-depth: -
A determination by the senior agency official that a facility's security program consists of layered and complementary security controls sufficient to deter, detect, and document unauthorized entry and movement within a facility. Uses active and passive complementary physical security measures.

Point Security-
For the US Constitution and an installation (guarding a specific asset).

Area Security-
For Pentagon and installation (protects entire facility/installation).

PIE-FAO (Identify assets)-
People, Information, Equipment, Facilities, Activities, Operations

Identify Threats-
Foreign Intel Agents, Terrorists, Foreign Military, Criminals, Civil Disturbances, Insider Threats, Environmental Threats, Cyber Threats

Foreign Intel Agent Threats-
Adversaries acting in the interest of a foreign intelligence entity that actively engages in intel activities against the US or its assets.

Terrorist Threats-
Adversaries who use violence or the threat of violence to instill fear with the intent to coerce or intimidate governments or societies in the pursuit of goals that are generally political, religious, or ideological

Foreign Military Forces Threats-
Four elements in this structure: leaders, active cadre, active supporters, passive supporters.

Criminal Threats-
Adversaries who commit crimes against people or property such as assault/theft/hacking.

Civil Disturbance Threats-
Most often arise from political grievances, urban economic conflicts, community unrest, terrorist acts, of foreign influences. They can range from peaceful picketing to full-blown riot situations.

Insider Threats-
Trusted persons who have been granted access to DoD resources or services.

Environmental Threats-
Natural phenomena/disasters that have the potential to damage DoD resources or services or interrupt activities/operations.

Cyber Threats-
Attacks on DoD computer systems and information contained in those systems.

What is a threat? -
An indication, circumstance, or event with the potential to cause loss of, or damage to, an asset or capability.

Vulnerabilities-
Weaknesses, characteristics, or circumstances that can be exploited by an adversary to gain access to or information from an asset.

Examples of Vulnerabilities-
Building construction
Location of people/equip
Operational practices
Personal Behavior

Conduct Risk Analysis-
Consider impact and likelihood - loss of strategic or military advantage or loss of life.

Determine Countermeasures-
Reduce Vulnerabilities & mitigate threats: facility design, day-to-day operations, when threats increase

Make Risk Management Decision-
Cost analysis/Benefit analysis

E.O 10421 (1952)-
Providing Physical Security or Facilities Important to the National Defense

E.O. 11051 (1962)-
Prescribing Responsibilities of the Office of Emergency Planning in the Executive Office of the President

E.O. 12148 (1979)-
Federal Emergency Management

E.O. 12656 (1988)-
Assignment of Emergency Preparedness Responsibilities

Attack on Khobar Towers (1996)-
SecDef accepted responsibility for AT/FP in DoD. Designates CJCS as focal point for all DoD.

Homeland Security Act of 2002-
Signed as a result of Sept 11, 2001 attacks.

E.O. 13228-
Establishing the Office of Homeland Security and the Homeland Security Council

HSPD-12 (2004)-
Policy for Common ID Standard for Federal/Contractor Employees

E.O. 13231-
Critical Infrastructure Protection in the Information Age

E.O. 13636 (2013)-
Improving Critical Infrastructure Cybersecurity

PPD-21 (2013)-
Critical Infrastructure Security and Resilience

DoDI 5200.08 - Security of DoD Installations and Resources and the DoD Physical Security Review Board (PSRB)-
Authorizes commanders to issue regulations for the protection of property and places under their command.
Builds consistent minimum standards for protecting DoD installations and resources

DoD 5200.08-R Physical Security Program-
Implements DoD Policies and minimum standards for the physical protections of DoD assets

DoDM 5200.01 Volumes 1-4: DoD Information Security Program-
Addresses the physical security aspects of protecting classified information

Installation Commander/Facility Director-
Responsible for the safety and protection of people and property.
Physical security planning, coordination, and integration.
Identification of mission essential capabilities.

Antiterrorism Officer (ATO)-
Manages the installation or facility antiterrorism program.
Using defensive measures to reduce vulnerability of individuals and property from terrorist attacks.

Counterintelligence (CI) Support Personnel-
Providing information on the capabilities, intentions, and threats of adversaries.
Paying close attention to adversaries associated with foreign intelligence entities.
Assessing counterintelligence considerations in support of physical security program.

Law Enforcement Personnel-
Effective liaison with local, state, and federal law enforcement officials
Coordinating support for: supporting antiterrorism concerns and efforts, supporting emergency response, addressing criminal incidents

OPSEC Officer-
Identify critical information.
Identify threats to specific assets.
Asses vulnerabilities to assets.
Analyze risk to specific assets and national security.
Develop countermeasures against potential threats to national security and other DoD assets.

Physical Security Officer-

Manages, implements, directs physical security programs.
Develops and maintaining physical security plans, instructions, regulations, and standard policies and procedures.
Coordinating with local law enforcement agencies, antiterrorism officers, and loss prevention personnel.

Physical Security Coordinating Activities-
ATEC/ATWG/TWG/MA SSG

Antiterrorism Executive Committee (ATEC) - DoDI 2000.12 AT Program-
Develops and refines AT program guidance, policy, standards.
Acting on recommendations of ATWG/TWG to: determine resource allocation priorities, mitigate terrorism-related vulnerabilities
Integrate and align AT and mission assurance efforts

Antiterrorism Working Group (ATWG)-
Assessing requirements for physical security.
Recommendations and developing policy.
Preparing planning documents.
Conducting criticality, vulnerability, and risk assessments.

What is the ATWG comprised of? -
Antiterrorism Officer (ATO)
Representatives from all appropriate commands, organizations, and tenant activities

Threat Working Group (TWG) responsibilities: -
Identifying threats
Informing installation CO on current threats

TWG is comprised of: -
ATO
CI Representative
Law enforcement rep
OPSEC officer
Information Operations rep
CBRNE rep

Mission Assurance Senior Steering Group (MA SSG): -
Provides advocacy, coordination, and oversight in MA alignment efforts on issues that cut across all DoD protection programs.
Functions as Office of SecDef and Joint Staff-level management and decision support forum.

MA SSG is comprised of: -
Senior Executive Service and general or flag officers at the 1 and 2-star levels

Physical Security Site Design Considerations-
Obstacles(waterways/ditches).
Warning Signs
Lighting

Military Working Dogs
Barriers and Fencing
Gate/Guard

Restricted Areas-
Require additional protection
Limit access to authorized personnel
Are designated to safeguard property or material; by facility directors or installation commanders
Improve security
Provide additional layers of security

Type of barriers: -
Fences (made of chain link/barbed wire/concertina)
Fences and barriers are the first line of defense/establish boundaries/deter unauthorized entry/used as platforms for sensors/prevent unwanted observation.

Types of Site Lighting: -
Continuous - series of fixed lights to flood an area with overlapping cones of light
Standby - lamps are NOT continuous lit; used when additional lighting is necessary
Emergency - Depends on alternative power sources
Movable - When supplemental lighting is necessary

Purpose of site lighting: -
Enables guards to observe activities inside and around an installation
Discourages unauthorized entry
Reveals persons within an area
Supplements other protective measures

Security Forces are comprised of: -
DoD Civ/Mil/Contractor/Mil working dogs

Security Forces Responsibilities: -
Protect areas such as static observation posts/access control points.
Serve as roving patrols/response forces/security system monitors/dispatchers in control centers/escorts

Interior Intrusion Detection System (IDS) Purpose: -
Deter/detect/document/deny/delay intrusion

Types of Interior IDS: -
Volumetric detectors - detect change in particular area/active and passive
Operable opening switches - used on doors & windows/work with magnetic switch. balances magnetic switch (BMS) or high security switch (HSS)
Interior barrier protectors - protect against amateur intruders/use infrared beam or trip wire
Proximity detectors - provide point security/composed of pressure mat and capacitance detector

Exterior IDS include: -
Fence disturbance sensors - detect disturbances of the fence
Invisible barrier detection - detect motion specific area/use microwave or infrared

Buried line sensors - detect vibrations or pressure changes/buries in ground
Electric field sensors - contain multiple wires/alarm will activate when energy in wire is disturbed

Closed Circuit Television (CCTV) system: -
Captures visual image/transmits image to remote location - image can be displayed, recorded, and printed

Reasons to use CCTV: -
Deter and detect loss, theft, or misuse
Monitor multiple areas simultaneously
Are cost effective

Access Control System-
Prevents entry by unauthorized personnel
Are one of the INNER layers of security-in-depth
Are based on risk management
Range from manual to automatic and electronic

Access Control System (manual)-
Non-electronic cipher access control device

Access Control System (automated)-
Electronic cipher access control device (card reader/proximity card ready/keypad/wireless sensor)

Access Control System (manual, using automated electronics)-
Common Access Card

Access Control System (automated)-
Biometric access control device (fingerprints/hand geometry/handwriting/iris scan/voice recognition)

Screening Equipment types: -
X-ray machine
Portable, hand-held metal detectors
Permanently installed metal detectors
Other specialized equipment

Two-way radio-
Serves as primary means of communication between - response forces
Should have back-up communications systems read in case of radio failure

Identification Systems (Methods)-
Verify your identity
Protect our national security and other DoD assets
Vary when accessing different areas

Types of entry control methods: -
Personal recognition
Automated entry control systems

Exchange badge systems
Guard personnel conducting physical inspections of identification

Methods of Control-
Escorts/access control rosters/badging system/two-person concept

Entry/Exit Inspections-
Criteria are determined by installation and facility authorities: frequency (100% random)/upon entry and/or exit
Are conducted to screen for: illegal and prohibited articles upon entry/unauthorized removal of government assets upon exit
Serve as deterrent
Detect contraband

Types of Locks-
Combination (electromechanical/mechanical/padlock)
Key Operated (high security padlock/low security padlock/mortise lock)

Electromechanical Locks-
Approved for classified storage
Kaba Mas X-07/8/9/10, CDX-07/8/9/10
S&G 2740, 2740B, 2890PDL
Meets FF-L-2740 series lock specification

Mechanical Locks-
S&G 2937
Meets prior standards
May be approved for classified storage of S and C information

Padlock-
S&G 8077/AD
Approved for storage of S or C bulk or temporary indoor storage
Meets FF-P-110 series lock specification

High Security Padlock-
S&G 833C, 951
Approved for high security protection

Low Security Padlock-
Secondary Locks
Provides limited-to-minimal resistance to forced or surreptitious entry

Mortise Lock-
Provides low security
Cylindrical and deadbolt

Key Access and Control Measures-
Vary based on the program or regulatory requirements

Should include: key register/list of authorized personnel
Protect DoD assets

Storage Methods (large volumes of classified)-
Secure Rooms/vaults/SCIFs

Secure Rooms-
For open Storage of classified information
Built to commercial construction standards

Vaults-
Built to meet strict forcible entry standards
Key characteristics: reinforced concrete walls, ceiling, floor/hardened steel door
SCIFs: for storage of SCI/built to strict standards/Intel Community (IC) tech spec for ICD/ICS 705 provides construction information

Security Containers-
Used to store classified information, they must:
Be approved by GSA/Have locking devices that meet GSA standards/NOT be used to store other items with classified information

Physical Security Plan (PSP)-
Comprehensive written plans providing for appropriate economical use of personnel and equipment to prevent or minimize criminal or disruptive activities.

PSPs should include: -
Special and general guard orders/access and material control/protective barrier and lighting systems/locks/IDS
May be designated as FOUO or Classified

Standard Operating Procedures (SOPs): -
Provide supplemental guidance for physical security programs
Establish procedures for emergency events
Establish operational and administrative procedures

Post Orders-
Establish duties/roles/responsibilities at:
Individual assignments
Checkpoints
Gates
Guard posts

Inspections serve to: -
Ensure compliance with physical security plan
Verify policy compliance
Promote cost-effective security
Serve as an opportunity for security education
Establish and/or enhance good working relationships

Identify existing or potential program weaknesses
Promote quality performance of security functions

Compliance Inspections-
Ensure regulatory requirements are being met
Are conducted by senior official
Examples: assist visits/command/inspections/IG inspections

Self-Inspections-
Are conducted by members of your organization
Usually with aid of checklist
May aid internal control
Prepare for compliance inspections
Ensure physical security program is cost-effective

Physical Security Measures: -
Detection/deterrence/delay/denial/notification

Threat Levels-
High - anti-US terrorists are operationally active and use large casualty-producing attacks as preferred method
Significant - anti-US terrorists are present and attack personnel as their preferred method of operation
Moderate - Terrorists are present but no indications of anti-US activity
Low - no terrorist group detected

FPCONs-
Actions taken to prevent or mitigate hostile actions against DoD, to include: personnel (& family)/resources/facilities/critical information

Commanders' responsibilities regarding AT/FP: -
Implement FPCON
Remind personnel to be alert for and report suspicious activities
Educate personnel on the insider threat
Comply with and integrate access control policies into their FPCON plans
Augment FPCON measures as necessary

The two primary purposes of physical security are protection and?

a. Security-in-depth
b. Prevention
c. Point Security
d. Area Security

b. Prevention

A guard checking IDs at the gate of an installation is a good example of what type of security?

a. Security-in-depth

b. Prevention
c. Point Security
d. Area Security

c. Point Security

_____ is the layering of physical security countermeasures such as fencing, guards, cameras, lighting, and locks.

a. Security-in-depth
b. Prevention
c. Point Security
d. Area Security

   a. Security-in-depth

Before you can conduct a risk analysis, based on the impact and likelihood of an unwanted event happening, what steps in the risk management process must you take first?

a. Identify assets
b. Identify threats
c. Determine countermeasure options
d. Identify vulnerabilities
e. Make risk management decisions

A, B, & D

Which policy guidance would you consult to find the minimum standards for the physical protection of DoD assets?

A. DoD 5200.08-R, Physical Security Program
B. DoDI 5200.08, Security of DoD Installations and Resources and the DoD Physical Security Review Board (PSRB)
C. DoDM 5200.01, Volumes 1-4 DoD Information Security Program

A. DoD 5200.08-R, Physical Security Program

Which policy should you consult to find the physical security requirements of protecting classified information?

a. DoD 5200.08-R, Physical Security Program
b. DoDI 5200.08, Security of DoD Installations and Resources and the DoD Physical Security Review Board (PSRB)
c. DoDM 5200.01, Volumes 1-4 DoD Information Security Program

C. DoDM 5200.01, Volumes 1-4 DoD Information Security Program

Which policy authorizes commanders to issue regulations for the protection or security of property and places under their command?

a. DoD 5200.08-R, Physical Security Program
b. DoDI 5200.08, Security of DoD Installations and Resources and the DoD Physical Security Review Board (PSRB)
c. DoDM 5200.01, Volumes 1-4 DoD Information Security Program

B. DoDI 5200.08, Security of DoD Installations and Resources and the DoD Physical Security Review Board (PSRB)

Who is charged with management, implementation, and direction of all physical security programs?

a. Law Enforcement
b. Antiterrorism Officer
c. OPSEC Officer
d.CI Support
e. Physical Security Officer

e. Physical Security Officer

Who is responsible for providing valuable information on the capabilities, intentions, and threats of adversaries?

a. Law Enforcement
b. Antiterrorism Officer
c. OPSEC Officer
d.CI Support
e. Physical Security Officer

d. CI Support

Who is responsible for developing countermeasures against potential threats to national security and other DoD assets?

a. Law Enforcement
b. Antiterrorism Officer
c. OPSEC Officer
d.CI Support
e. Physical Security Officer

c. OPSEC Officer

Which of the following individuals should be included in a Threat Working Group?

a. Antiterrorism Officer
b. Counterintelligence (CI) representative
c. Law enforcement representative

d. Operations security officer

e. Information operations representative)

f. Chemical, biological, radiological, nuclear and high yield explosive representative

All are Correct

Which of these can be made of solid steel to make them more attack resistant?

a. walls
b. doors
c. windows
d. roofs

b. doors

Which of these house ventilation systems that should be secured with steel bars?

a. walls
b. doors
c. windows
d. roofs

d. roofs

Which of these should be covered with a protective film to make them less dangerous in an attack?

a. walls
b. doors
c. windows
d. roofs

c. windows

Which of the following locks are approved to secure classified information or material?

a. Kaba Mas X-10
b. S&G 8077/AD
c. S&G 833 C

A & B

True or False. Standby lighting is used when regular lighting is not available

False

True or False. Site lighting is used to enable guard force personnel to observe activities inside or outside the installation

True

True or False. Movable lighting is used when supplemental lighting is needed such as at construction sites.

True

At a minimum _____ should include special and general guard orders, access and material control, protective barriers, lighting systems, locks, and Intrusion Detection Systems (IDS).

a. Standard Operating Procedures
b. Physical Security Plans
c. Post Orders

b. physical security plans

_____ establish duties, roles, and responsibilities at individual assignments, checkpoints, gates, and guard posts.

a. Standard Operating Procedures
b. Physical Security Plans
c. Post Orders

c. post orders

_____provide supplemental guidance for physical security programs and establish procedures for emergency events as well as operational and administrative procedures.

a. Standard Operating Procedures
b. Physical Security Plans
c. Post Orders

a. Standard Operating Procedures

True or False. Commanders may only implement measures according to the FPCON level in force at the time.

False

True or False. Commanders must comply with and integrate DoD physical security and installation access control policies into their FPCON plans.

True

True or False. Commanders educate their personnel on the insider threat to DoD elements and personnel.

True

Designation of a restricted area is the responsibility of the Physical Security Director.

a. True
b. False

b. False

A restricted area must be properly marked to inform personnel that they are in the vicinity of a restricted area.

a. True
b. False

a. True

All individuals with the appropriate personnel clearance level are allowed access to a designated restricted area.

a. True
b. False

b. False

Controlled areas may be set up adjacent to designated Restricted Areas to facilitate the verification and authentication of personnel.

a. True
b. False

a. True

Restricted areas employ physical security measures to prevent unauthorized entry and/or minimize incursions or interference.

a. True
b. False

a. True

Restricted areas may be of different types depending on the nature and varying degree of importance of the security interest.

a. True
b. False

a. True

Only the installation Commander or the Activity Director can authorize a restricted area.

a. True
b. False

a. True

Two security professionals - Jo and Chris - are discussing Facility Access Control Procedures.

Jo says that admittance to a restricted area is typically limited to personnel assigned to the area and persons who have been specifically authorized access to that area.

Chris says that visitors to a restricted area must be escorted by personnel assigned to the area or by persons who have been specifically authorized access to that area.

Who is correct?
a. Jo is correct
b. Chris is correct
c. Jo and Chris are both correct
d. Jo and Chris are both incorrect

c. Jo and Chris are both correct

This facility access control procedure includes procedures for searching packages, vehicles, and personnel.

a. Identification Systems and Methods
b. Methods of Control
c. Entry and Exit Inspection

c. Entry and Exit Inspection

The facility access control procedure employs various types of entry control devices including the use of the Common Access Card.

a. Identification Systems and Methods
b. Methods of Control
c. Entry and Exit Inspection

a. Identification Systems and Methods

This facility access control procedure employs the use of physical security countermeasures including automated entry control systems, exchange badge systems, and security personnel conducting physical inspection of your
credentials.

a. Identification Systems and Methods
b. Methods of Control

c. Entry and Exit Inspection

a. Identification Systems and Methods

This facility access control procedure employs escorts and access control rosters to ensure accountability for all visitors to an area.

a. Identification Systems and Methods
b. Methods of Control
c. Entry and Exit Inspection

b. Methods of Control

The two-person concept requiring two people to be present at all times while in a defined area is an example of this facility access control procedure.

a. Identification Systems and Methods
b. Methods of Control
c. Entry and Exit Inspection

b. Methods of Control

The use of an x-ray machine or metal detector to determine whether or not a person is bringing unauthorized items into an area is an example of this facility access control.

a. Identification Systems and Methods
b. Methods of Control
c. Entry and Exit Inspection

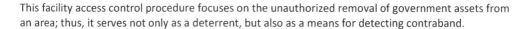

c. Entry and Exit Inspection

This facility access control procedure focuses on the unauthorized removal of government assets from an area; thus, it serves not only as a deterrent, but also as a means for detecting contraband.

a. Identification Systems and Methods
b. Methods of Control
c. Entry and Exit Inspection

c. Entry and Exit Inspection

The Homeland Security Presidential Directive 12 (HSPD 12) aims to reduce the number of systems used in this facility access control procedures by mandating common system criteria.

a. Identification Systems and Methods
b. Methods of Control
c. Entry and Exit Inspection

a. Identification Systems and Methods

The use of different badges for visitors in an example of this facility access control procedure.

a. Identification Systems and Methods
b. Methods of Control
c. Entry and Exit Inspection

b. Methods of Control

Two security professionals - Jo and Chris - are discussing Facility Access Control Procedures.

Jo says that, within the Department of Defense, the Common Access Card fulfills the requirements of the common identification criteria mandated by HSPD 12.

Chris says that, depending on the area sensitivity some Department of Defense facilities may still require credentials in addition to the Common Access Card as part of their facility access control procedure.

Who is correct?
a. Jo is correct
b. Chris is correct
c. Jo and Chris are both correct
d. Jo and Chris are both incorrect

c. Jo and Chris are both correct

Two security professionals - Jo and Chris- are discussing lock systems typically used within the Department of Defense (DoD).

Jo says that the two primary types of locks used within DoD are combination locks and key operated locks.

Chris says that the type of locking device selected for use depends on the environment and the type of assets that require protection.

Who is correct?
a. Jo is correct
b. Chris is correct
c. Jo and Chris are both correct
d. Jo and Chris are both incorrect

c. Jo and Chris are both correct

Mortise locks are considered low security locking devices typically found in general office areas.

a. True
b. False

a. True

The two types of combination locks approved for use to safeguard classified information includes a family of locks known as X-07, X-08, X-09; and combination padlocks that comply with an Underwriters' Laboratory Standard.

a. True
b. False

a. True

Low security padlocks provide limited-to-minimal resistance to forced or surreptitious entry.

a. True
b. False

a. True

Lock and Key control procedures should include a key register and an authorized user list.

a. True
b. False

a. True

Key control procedures are necessary because corrective measures associated with lost or uncontrolled keys can be costly and time consuming.

a. True
b. False

a. True

Locks used to secure classified information must meet FF-L-2740 specifications.

a. True
b. False

a. True

Two security professionals - Jo and Chris- are discussing the Department of Defense's (DoD) Physical Security Program.

Jo says that the DoD Physical Security Program uses active and passive measures to detect, deter, delay, and/or deny unauthorized access to personnel, installations, equipment, facilities, activities, and operations.

Chris says that one purpose of the DoD Physical Security Program is to prevent damage to the theft of, and/or loss of the Department assets.

Who is correct?
a. Jo is correct
b. Chris is correct
c. Jo and Chris are both correct
d. Jo and Chris are both incorrect

c. Jo and Chris are both correct

Two security professionals - Jo and Chris - are discussing the Department of Defense (DoD) Physical Security Program.

Jo says that physical security uses active and passive measures to safeguard personnel, installations, equipment, facilities, activities, and operations against espionage, sabotage, terrorism, damage, and criminal activity.

Chris says that prevention and protection are the primary purposes of a physical security program.

Who is correct?
a. Jo is correct
b. Chris is correct
c. Jo and Chris are both correct
d. Jo and Chris are both incorrect

c. Jo and Chris are both correct

To achieve security-in-depth, a security program needs to employ and deploy layers of complementary security controls to deter, detect, delay, assess, respond, and document unauthorized movement within the facility.

a. True
b. False

a. True

A security program determined to have security-in-depth employs an integrated protective system of active and passive security controls.

a. True
b. False

a. True

Security-in-depth is a security concept that calls for the systematic use of physical security measures in levels or steps to create different layers of protection.

a. True
b. False

a. True

Because different assets may require different levels of protection, the security in depth concept calls for the use of different types of security controls to ensure that each asset has the same level protection.

a. True
b. False

b. False

This entity manages, implements, and directs the installation or facility's physical security program.

a. Anti-Terrorism Working Group (ATWG)
b. Anti-Terrorism Officer
c. CI Support Personnel
d. Force Protection Working Group (FPWG)
e. Information Systems Security Managers (ISSM)
f. Installation Commander/Facility Director
g. Law Enforcement Officials
h. Legal Officers
i. Operations Security Officer
j. Physical Security Officer/Provost Marshal
k. Threat Working Group (TWG)

j. Physical Security Officer/Provost Marshal

This entity has overall responsibility for the safety and protection of the people and property in an installation or a facility.

a. Anti-Terrorism Working Group (ATWG)
b. Anti-Terrorism Officer
c. CI Support Personnel
d. Force Protection Working Group (FPWG)
e. Information Systems Security Managers (ISSM)
f. Installation Commander/Facility Director
g. Law Enforcement Officials
h. Legal Officers
i. Operations Security Officer
j. Physical Security Officer/Provost Marshal
k. Threat Working Group (TWG)

f. Installation Commander/Facility Director

This entity is responsible for assessing physical security requirements and for conducting criticality, vulnerability, and risk assessments.

a. Anti-Terrorism Working Group (ATWG)
b. Anti-Terrorism Officer
c. CI Support Personnel
d. Force Protection Working Group (FPWG)
e. Information Systems Security Managers (ISSM)
f. Installation Commander/Facility Director
g. Law Enforcement Officials
h. Legal Officers
i. Operations Security Officer
j. Physical Security Officer/Provost Marshal
k. Threat Working Group (TWG)

a. Anti-Terrorism Working Group (ATWG)

This entity is responsible for ensuring the proper and legal incorporation of security considerations.

a. Anti-Terrorism Working Group (ATWG)
b. Anti-Terrorism Officer
c. CI Support Personnel
d. Force Protection Working Group (FPWG)
e. Information Systems Security Managers (ISSM)
f. Installation Commander/Facility Director
g. Law Enforcement Officials
h. Legal Officers
i. Operations Security Officer
j. Physical Security Officer/Provost Marshal
k. Threat Working Group (TWG)

h. Legal Officers

This entity is responsible for coordinating physical security measures to protect information systems.

a. Anti-Terrorism Working Group (ATWG)
b. Anti-Terrorism Officer
c. CI Support Personnel
d. Force Protection Working Group (FPWG)
e. Information Systems Security Managers (ISSM)
f. Installation Commander/Facility Director
g. Law Enforcement Officials
h. Legal Officers
i. Operations Security Officer
. Physical Security Officer/Provost Marshal
k. Threat Working Group (TWG)

e. Information Systems Security Managers (ISSM)

This entity supports the physical security mission by managing the installation's use of defensive measures to reduce the vulnerability of individuals and property
from terrorist attacks.

a. Anti-Terrorism Working Group (ATWG)
b. Anti-Terrorism Officer
c. CI Support Personnel
d. Force Protection Working Group (FPWG)
e. Information Systems Security Managers (ISSM)
f. Installation Commander/Facility Director
g. Law Enforcement Officials
h. Legal Officers
i. Operations Security Officer
j. Physical Security Officer/Provost Marshal
k. Threat Working Group (TWG)

b. Anti-Terrorism Officer

This entity supports the physical security mission by providing information on our adversaries' intentions and capabilities.

a. Anti-Terrorism Working Group (ATWG)
b. Anti-Terrorism Officer
c. CI Support Personnel
d. Force Protection Working Group (FPWG)
e. Information Systems Security Managers (ISSM)
f. Installation Commander/Facility Director
g. Law Enforcement Officials
h. Legal Officers
i. Operations Security Officer
j. Physical Security Officer/Provost Marshal
k. Threat Working Group (TWG)

c. CI Support Personnel

This entity supports the physical security mission by facilitating the identification of critical information.

a. Anti-Terrorism Working Group (ATWG)
b. Anti-Terrorism Officer
c. CI Support Personnel
d. Force Protection Working Group (FPWG)
e. Information Systems Security Managers (ISSM)
f. Installation Commander/Facility Director
g. Law Enforcement Officials
h. Legal Officers
i. Operations Security Officer
j. Physical Security Officer/Provost Marshal

k. Threat Working Group (TWG)

i. Operations Security Officer

Two Security Professionals - Jo and Chris- are discussing physical security threats.

Jo says that natural disasters are considered a physical security threat because they have the potential to damage DoD resources or interrupt activities or operations.

Chris says that, although natural disasters have the potential to damage DoD resources or interrupt activities or operations, they are not considered a physical security threat because they are natural occurring phenomena.

Who is correct?
a. Jo is correct
b. Chris is correct
c. Jo and Chris are both correct
d. Jo and Chris are both incorrect

b. Chris is correct

Which of the following is an adversary who uses the threat of violence to instill fear and intimidate governments to fulfill goals that are generally political, religious, or ideological?

a. Criminal
b. Foreign Intelligence Agents
c. Insider
d. Terrorists

d. Terrorists

Which of the following is an adversary that actively engages in intelligence activities against the U.S. in the interest of another country?

a. Criminal
b. Foreign Intelligence Security Service
c. Insider
d. Terrorists

b. Foreign Intelligence Security Service

This concept refers to an indication, circumstance, or event with the potential to cause loss of or damage to an asset.

a. Criticality
b. Threat
c. Vulnerability

b. Threat

This concept refers to a situation or circumstance, which if left unchanged, may result in damage to mission-essential resources.

a. Criticality
b. Threat
c. Vulnerability

c. Vulnerability

This concept refers to weaknesses that can be exploited by an adversary to gain unauthorized access to or information from an asset.

a. Criticality
b. Threat
c. Vulnerability

c. Vulnerability

This concept refers to the perceived imminence of intended aggression by a capable entity to harm a government's programs, operations, people, installations, or facilities.

a. Criticality
b. Threat
c. Vulnerability

b. Threat

This concept looks at the importance of a part to the whole.

a. Criticality
b. Threat
c. Vulnerability

a. Criticality

This concept is based on both an asset's importance to national security, and the effect of its partial or complete loss.

a. Criticality
b. Threat
c. Vulnerability

a. Criticality

Two Security Professionals - Jo and Chris- are discussing the physical security principles of point and area security.

Jo says that area security maximizes the effectiveness of response forces by focusing security efforts on a specific asset or resource.

Chris says that only point security allows a security professional to effectively protect assets from damage, loss, and theft.

Who is correct?
a. Jo is correct
b. Chris is correct
c. Jo and Chris are both correct
d. Jo and Chris are both incorrect

d. Jo and Chris are both incorrect

Two security professionals- Jo and Chris- are discussing the physical security principles of point and area security.

Jo says that point security is a physical security principle that calls for the use of a physical security measure to protect a consolidated set of assets.

Chris says that area security is a physical security principle that calls for the use of a consolidated set of physical security measures to protect a specific asset or resource.

Who is correct?
a. Jo is correct
b. Chris is correct
c. Jo and Chris are both correct
d. Jo and Chris are both incorrect

d. Jo and Chris are both incorrect

Two security professionals - Jo and Chris- are discussing the physical security principles of point and area security.

Jo says that security professionals employ both point and area security to protect assets from damage, loss, and theft.

Chris says that security professionals employ both point and area security in an integrated manner to protect national security.

Who is correct?
a. Jo is correct
b. Chris is correct
c. Jo and Chris are both correct
d. Jo and Chris are both incorrect

c. Jo and Chris are both correct

Two security professionals - Jo and Chris- are discussing threat levels and Force Protection Conditions (FPCON).

Jo says that the FPCON level set by authorized personnel dictates the security measures an installation enacts to prevent or mitigate hostile actions against its personnel, resources, facilities, and critical information.

Chris says that senior leaders use threat levels to assist them in determining the appropriate FPCON level.

Who is correct?
a. Jo is correct
b. Chris is correct
c. Jo and Chris are both correct
d. Jo and Chris are both incorrect

c. Jo and Chris are both correct

Which of the following threat levels suggest that there are terrorists present but there are no indications of anti-U.S. activity?

a. Low
b. Moderate
c. Significant
d. High

b. Moderate

Which of the following FPCON levels indicates the existence of an increased threat of terrorist activity?

a. FPCON ALPHA
b. FPCON BRAVO
c. FPCON CHARLIE
d. FPCON DELTA

c. FPCON CHARLIE

Two security professionals - Jo and Chris- are discussing Crime Prevention Programs.

Jo says that the Department of Defense (DoD) considers criminals a threat because they have the potential to cause the loss of or damage to DoD assets or operations.

Chris says that crime prevention is a DoD Physical Security Program goal.

Who is correct?
a. Jo is correct
b. Chris is correct

c. Jo and Chris are both correct
d. Jo and Chris are both incorrect

c. Jo and Chris are both correct

The first layer of an integrated physical security system typically uses protective barriers to protect a facility's perimeter.

a. True
b. False

a. True

The perimeter of an installation or facility is the outermost area of security responsibility for physical security practitioners.

a. True
b. False

a. True

Protective barriers such as poured concrete or hardened steel barriers are used for establishing perimeter boundaries.

a. True
b. False

a. True

Protective barriers deter individuals from attempting unlawful or unauthorized entry.

a. True
b. False

a. True

Protective barriers such as fencing can also be used as platforms for sensors and lighting.

a. True
b. False

a. True

Two security professionals- Jo and Chris- are discussing protective barriers.

Jo says that protective barriers can be used to enforce facility access control.

Chris says that protective barriers can be used to harden a facility.

Who is correct?
a. Jo is correct
b. Chris is correct
c. Jo and Chris are both correct
d. Jo and Chris are both incorrect

c. Jo and Chris are both correct

Secure rooms and vaults are areas designated and authorized for the open storage of classified information.

a. True
b. False

a. True

Vaults are different from secure rooms in that vaults typically meet SCIF construction requirements.

a. True
b. False

b. False

Vaults have reinforced concrete on walls, ceilings, and floors, and have a hardened steel door.

a. True
b. False

a. True

SCIFs are designed to store sensitive compartmented information - information that requires enhanced protection exceeding those normally required for information at the same level of classification.

a. True
b. False

True

Secure rooms and vaults must be constructed to meet GSA-approved standards.

a. True
b. False

b. False

Vaults and SCIFs must be constructed based on standards set in DCID 6/9.

a. True
b. False

b. False

GSA approves security containers used to store classified information.

a. True
b. False

a. True

Secure rooms are usually built to commercial standards and provide a similar level of protection as a vault.

a. True
b. False

b. False

Two security professionals - Jo and Chris- are discussing access control systems.

Jo says that the choice of which access control system- manual or automated-to use should be determined based on an analysis of the criticality, vulnerability, and the threat to the asset requiring protection.

Chris says that access control is one of the inner layers in a security-in-depth approach to physical security.

Who is correct?
a. Jo is correct
b. Chris is correct
c. Jo and Chris are both correct
d. Jo and Chris are both incorrect

c. Jo and Chris are both correct

Access control systems are implemented to prevent unauthorized personnel from entering a designated area.

a. True
b. False

a. True

An example of a manual access control system is a stand-alone system that requires the user to know a 3- or 4-digit number to gain access to the designated area.

a. True
b. False

a. True

An example of a manual system that uses automated electronics is the common access card that allows users to authenticate signatures, securely log onto computer systems, and gain access into designated areas.

a. True
b. False

a. True

Biometric access control systems use individually unique characteristics such as fingerprints and voice to authenticate that an individual is authorized to gain access onto a designated area.

a. True
b. False

a. True

Two security professionals- Jo and Chris- are discussing intrusion detection systems (IDS)

Jo says that an IDS uses sensors, control units, transmission line, and monitor units to detect a change in the environment.

Chris says that the two types of IDS are active and passive.

Who is correct?
a. Jo is correct
b. Chris is correct
c. Jo and Chris are both correct
d. Jo and Chris are both incorrect

a. Jo is correct

Two security professionals -Jo and Chris- are discussing intrusion detection systems (IDS).

Jo says that IDS can be used for area security.

Chris says that IDS can be used for point security.

Who is correct?
a. Jo is correct
b. Chris is correct
c. Jo and Chris are both correct
d. Jo and Chris are both incorrect

a. Jo is correct

CCTV is considered cost effective because it allows security personnel to monitor multiple areas simultaneously.

a. True
b. False

a. True

CCTV systems consist of sensors, control units, transmission lines, and monitor units.

a. True
b. False

b. False

CCTV systems are used to prevent, deter, and detect pilferage.

a. True
b. False

a. True

CCTV systems allow security personnel to safely access and determine the size and intention of an unauthorized intrusion.

a. True
b. False

a. True

CCTV systems provide security personnel the capability to detect, identify, track, access, record, and coordinate response to unauthorized intrusions.

a. True
b. False

a. True

Two security professionals - Jo and Chris- are discussing screening equipment.

Jo says that screening equipment is used in facility access control procedures.

Chris says that the use of screening equipment includes the use of two-way radios as a way for response forces to communicate with their respective control centers.

Who is correct?
a. Jo is correct
b. Chris is correct
c. Jo and Chris are both correct
d. Jo and Chris are both incorrect

a. Jo is correct

Site lighting enables guard force personnel to observe activities inside and around an installation.

a. True
b. False

a. True

Site lighting discourages or deters attempts of unauthorized entry.

a. True
b. False

a. True

Site lighting plays a large part in physical security, but its use should supplement other protective measures such as fixed security posts or patrols, fences, and alarms.

a. True
b. False

a. True

Use of standby lighting is reserved for when regular lighting is not available.

a. True
b. False

b. False

Use of emergency lighting is reserved for situations when additional lighting is necessary.

a. True
b. False

b. False

Continuous lighting consists of a series of fixed lights arranged to continuously flood an area with overlapping cones of light.

a. True

b. False

a. True